Orlando

& Walt Disney World®

DIRECTIONS

WRITTEN AND RESEARCHED BY

Ross Velton

ROUGH GUIDES

NEW YORK • LONDON • DELHI

www.roughguides.com

Contents

Introduction to

Orlando

Since a certain animator chose its farmland as the Florida home for his theme parks, Orlando has become synonymous with Walt Disney World, and the sunny Disney vibe pumps relentlessly through the veins of this sprawling place. There's just no

▲ Disney's Animal Kingdom

way to avoid its impact – not that you necessarily want to. After all, while Orlando may hold all the trappings of an important city, with galleries, festivals, and the best nightlife in Central Florida, they serve more as a counterpoint; you're either here to escape into the fantasies that Disney, Universal Orlando, and other ancillary theme parks offer up or you're on the wrong vacation.

▲ Magic Kingdom

Walt Disney World is so large and spellbinding that it would be easy enough to spend several visits exploring its various attractions. Besides its four state-of-the-art theme parks – the signature Magic Kingdom, science-oriented EPCOT, Disney-MGM Studios, and the peerless Disney's Animal Kingdom – come

When to visit

Central Florida enjoys a pleasant year-round climate. The winters are generally mild, although occasional nighttime frosts do occur. Average temperatures in Orlando during this time are 61–67°F (16–19°C): very comfortable for touring the theme parks, but still a little chilly for the water parks. The temperatures and the humidity rise to hotter and stickier levels in the summer, when the thermometer hovers at 78–83°F (26–28°C); outside of the winter holidays, this is the busiest time of year in Orlando. January, May, and September are traditionally quieter months for the theme parks; however, convention-goers tend to fill the hotels in January, so a spring or early fall vacation is probably more ideal.

▲ Jurassic Park River Adventure

other superbly devised diversions, including two entertaining water parks and a modern sports complex. In short, Disney is escapism at its imaginative and psychological best.

Universal Orlando and SeaWorld Orlando, which followed in Disney's wake, were both quick to establish their own stellar reputations. Universal competes with Disney head-on, offering more white-knuckle thrill rides but a less magical atmosphere, while SeaWorld Orlando stands out as one of the country's best marine parks. Together the three destinations are the staples of most Orlando trips.

That hasn't stopped a bewildering number of other, lesser attractions from materializing to satisfy almost any whim or desire: you can swim with dolphins, throw hot-dogs at alligators, skydive, watch a rodeo, and even witness the resurrection of Christ – all for a price, of course. In the midst of this royal battle for the tourist dollar, it comes as a pleasant surprise to find some well-stocked museums and art galleries, several relaxing parks and lakes, and diverse cultural

▲ Discovery Cove

events in downtown Orlando and its northern suburbs. A visit there offers a glimpse into Orlando's unheralded sophistication – and provides the perfect antidote to theme-park burnout.

Sophistication can also be found in the city's fair share of gourmet restaurants and trendy urban eateries – though just as many visitors take advantage of the chain restaurants and inexpensive buffets blanketing the area. As for nightlife, downtown Orlando buzzes with a vibrant and eclectic after-dark scene; there are bars and clubs to suit all tastes.

▼ The Roxy nightclub in downtown Orlando

If you exhaust the parks and city (or get exhausted by them), the Kennedy Space Center, Tampa's theme park Busch Gardens, and the beach are all a short drive away. Wherever you go, you surely won't lack for entertainment.

Orlando
AT A GLANCE

Walt Disney World

This is why everyone comes to Orlando – and rightly so. Disney has no equal when it comes to fantasy-fulfillment, attention to detail, and revealing the child in us all. Its four main theme parks, full of amusement rides, wild animals, Disney characters, kids' shows, and stylized architecture, are the obvious draws, although a motor speedway, golf courses, resort hotels, and shops and restaurants galore offer something for everyone.

▲ Wishes fireworks at Cinderella Castle

Universal Orlando

While it may lack some of the magic of its nemesis Disney, Universal Orlando more than makes up for it with faster, edgier rides that appeal as much to grown-ups as to their offspring. Universal Studios offers a slew of memorable attractions based

on your favorite films; Islands of Adventure boasts Orlando's highest concentration of thrill rides; CityWalk is where the evening's entertainment takes place.

▲ Incredible Hulk Coaster

International Drive

This lively, garish drag is to Orlando what The Strip is to Las Vegas, lined with hotels, restaurants, and every attraction imaginable, including SeaWorld Orlando and Discovery Cove towards its southern end.

▼ Discovery Cove

▲ Shari Sushi restaurant in downtown Orlando

Downtown Orlando

Orlando's bustling downtown is in the midst of an exciting rejuvenation and well worth a visit, with trendy new bars and restaurants opening almost daily around Orange Avenue and in the chic Thornton Park district.

▼ Winter Park Farmers' Market

The northern suburbs

Museums and galleries, parks and lakes, and a strong sense of community characterize the small towns of Winter Park, Eatonville, and Maitland, just to the north of downtown Orlando.

Kissimmee

Beyond Orlando's southern city limit lies the town of Kissimmee, which clings proudly to its cowboy past with weekly rodeos, and offers some of Central Florida's most affordable accommodation.

Ideas

The big six

Most people come to Orlando to visit its renowned theme parks. The city does boast other worthwhile attractions, but the parks are by far the main draw. Each of the biggies has its own unique atmosphere, and it's quite possible to spend your entire vacation flitting from one magical land to another without ever seeing the other Orlando. Walt Disney World contributes four amazing parks to the mix, including the mother of all theme parks – the Magic Kingdom – and a zoo like you've never seen before, while Universal Orlando and Anheuser-Busch both feature two entertaining parks.

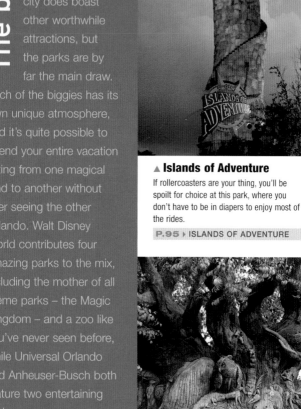

▲ Islands of Adventure

If rollercoasters are your thing, you'll be spoilt for choice at this park, where you don't have to be in diapers to enjoy most of the rides.

P.95 ▸ ISLANDS OF ADVENTURE

▲ Disney's Animal Kingdom

Only Disney could turn what is essentially a zoo into a wilderness park where you really feel like you're on an adventure in Asia and Africa.

P.72 ▸ DISNEY'S ANIMAL KINGDOM

▲ Universal Studios

Live out your favorite movie moments on cutting-edge rides at this park which doubles as a working production studio.

P.89 ▸ UNIVERSAL STUDIOS

▼ The Magic Kingdom

Very much the theme park for kids and kids-at-heart, the Kingdom's still casting its spell nearly forty years after opening.

P.51 ▸ THE MAGIC KINGDOM

▲ Discovery Cove

Enjoy VIP treatment and no crowds at this five-star park, where the main attraction is swimming with dolphins.

P.107 ▸ SEAWORLD ORLANDO AND DISCOVERY COVE

◄ SeaWorld Orlando

The animals are the stars at Florida's best marine park, especially when they take center stage in the entertaining live shows.

P.107 ▸ SEAWORLD ORLANDO AND DISCOVERY COVE

Music and dance

The performing arts scene in Orlando is unexpectedly vibrant, given the cultural prominence of the theme parks. Opera and ballet are both taken quite seriously, as is the classical music played at the long-running annual Bach Festival. Touring performers from many different musical genres usually make a stop at one of the city's several concert venues, while the renowned Cirque du Soleil have made Downtown Disney its permanent home.

▼ House of Blues

Enjoy blues, jazz, and soul performances in the concert hall, or gospel singers at Sunday brunch in the Southern-style restaurant.

P.87 ▸ DOWNTOWN DISNEY

▼ The Social

An intimate downtown concert venue with as much character as the alternative rock bands and other non-mainstream acts that play there.

P.129 ▸ DOWNTOWN ORLANDO

▲ Hard Rock Live

Check out such varied acts as Nelly or Willy Nelson at one of the city's best musical venues.

P.106 ▶ CITYWALK

▲ Cirque du Soleil

Spend a surreal night in the company of all-swinging, all-jumping, all-bending acrobats and gymnasts.

P.88 ▶ DOWNTOWN DISNEY

▲ Opera and ballet

The well-regarded Orlando Opera and Orlando Ballet each stage four or five shows a year.

P.129 ▶ DOWNTOWN ORLANDO

▶ Bach Festival

In late February and early March top orchestras and musicians come from all over to perform the works of Bach and other great composers.

P.174 ▶ ESSENTIALS

Adrenaline rush

The longest waiting lines are invariably for the rides that promise – and normally deliver – heart-pounding, nerve-jangling thrills and spills. With their massive frames towering hundreds of feet into the air, the rollercoasters are the most intimidating of these, although water slides and gravity-defying drops from great heights are equally effective at provoking screams.

▼ Rock 'n' Roller Coaster

The best rollercoaster Disney has to offer is made all the scarier by taking place in pitch blackness.

P.67 ▶ DISNEY-MGM STUDIOS

▼ Summit Plummet

The tallest and fastest water slide in the US is a virtual vertical drop, unmitigated by seats, harnesses, and other such reassurances.

P.78 ▶ THE REST OF WALT DISNEY WORLD

▲ The Twilight Zone Tower of Terror

Experience moments of weightlessness as you travel through The Fifth Dimension in a creepy hotel's service elevator.

P.67 ▸ DISNEY-MGM STUDIOS

▼ Kraken

Vertigo sufferers and those with weak constitutions will want to avoid this incredibly high, fast, and long rollercoaster.

P.110 ▸ SEAWORLD ORLANDO AND DISCOVERY COVE

◄ Dueling Dragons

Try to sit in the front row to get the full effect of the narrowly avoided collisions of these two "dueling" coasters.

P.98 ▸ ISLANDS OF ADVENTURE

Grown-up diversions

Touring the theme parks with children in tow can be mentally and physically draining. The kids' boundless energy combined with the type of rides that you'll be forced to go on will inevitably leave you pooped. Fortunately, there are opportunities in all the parks for grown-ups to indulge themselves every now and then. These diversions often come in the form of alcohol breaks, notably the free beer on offer at the Anheuser-Busch parks.

▲ Who Wants to Be a Millionaire – Play It!

This absorbing mock filming of the famous TV quiz show appeals to your competitive side by letting you test your general knowledge for a big prize.

P.67 ▶ DISNEY-MGM STUDIOS

▲ Richard Petty Driving Experience

Forget the rollercoasters – this ride around a NASCAR speedway in a stock-car is for hardcore speed junkies.

P.80 ▶ THE REST OF WALT DISNEY WORLD

◀ Anheuser-Busch Hospitality Center

Possibly the only freebie at a theme park just so happens to be beer at the Anheuser-Busch–owned SeaWorld Orlando and Busch Gardens.

P.111 ▸ SEAWORLD ORLANDO AND DISCOVERY COVE

▶ Sunbathing at the water parks

Sneak off to the deck chairs on the sandy beaches and relax while the kids wear themselves out on the slides.

P.78 ▸ THE REST OF WALT DISNEY WORLD

▾ Finnegan's Bar & Grill

This is the closest that any theme park restaurant comes to creating a party atmosphere for adults, due in part to the live music – but mostly the Guinness.

P.94 ▸ UNIVERSAL STUDIOS

Theme hotels

It is a testament to the seamless quality of Walt Disney World and its commitment to total escapism that leaving the theme parks at the end of the day does not necessarily mean the fantasy has to end. Numerous resort hotels dot the Disney parks, each with their own romantic ambience offering a pampered break from the stresses of daily life. Universal Orlando has followed suit in recent years and now offers its own themed resorts.

▲ Polynesian Resort

Sprawl out on the beach under palm trees at this imitation of a Polynesian beach hotel.

P.158 ▶ ACCOMMODATION

▲ Portofino Bay Hotel

Universal's delightful image of a quaint Italian seaside village comes with every comfort imaginable.

P.162 ▶ ACCOMMODATION

▼ Grand Floridian Resort & Spa

Disney's most luxurious hotel and spa is a throwback to what vacationing in Florida must have been like before the masses arrived.

P.158 ▸ ACCOMMODATION

▶ Animal Kingdom Lodge

Consider paying a little extra for the privilege of waking up in the morning and seeing African wildlife grazing outside your window.

P.159 ▸ ACCOMMODATION

▼ Wilderness Lodge

This peaceful log-cabin lodge with wood-burning fires feels worlds away from civilization.

P.158 ▸ ACCOMMODATION

▲ Double Tree Castle Hotel

One of the few theme hotels outside of Disney and Universal, this one takes the form of a turreted castle along International Drive.

P.162 ▸ ACCOMMODATION

Sports and outdoor activities

There is no question that the most popular sporting activity in Orlando is golf. You'll find five eighteen-hole courses on Disney property alone, and many other big resorts have their own courses. Other outdoor adventures include taking a ride in a hot-air balloon or exploring the countryside on a horse. At Disney's Wide World of Sports, you can watch a host of sporting events, both amateur and professional.

▲ Hot-air balloon trip

The ultimate bird's-eye view of Orlando is from a hot-air balloon.

P.143 ▸ SOUTH OF ORLANDO

▲ Disney's Wide World of Sports

You can watch everything from school soccer tournaments to the Atlanta Braves baseball team in spring training at this multifaceted sports venue.

P.79 ▸ THE REST OF WALT DISNEY WORLD

▶ Orlando Magic

Tickets are surprisingly affordable to watch Orlando's only major league professional sports team play basketball.

P.129 ▶ DOWNTOWN ORLANDO

▲ Daytona 500

The most prestigious NASCAR race of the year takes place in nearby Daytona Beach in February.

P.174 ▶ ESSENTIALS

▼ Golf

Orlando is a golfers' paradise, where every other green space seems to be a golf course.

P.176 ▶ ESSENTIALS

▲ Horseback riding

A sedate amble on horseback makes for a relaxing way of taking in the Orlando outdoors.

P.142 ▶ SOUTH OF ORLANDO

After dark

Although both Disney and Universal make a stab at offering hip nightlife venues, only downtown Orlando truly delivers appealing places to go after dark, from trendy lounges to dive bars. That said, many visitors forego the clubs in favor of staying on at the theme parks until closing time, when shows such as EPCOT's Illuminations: Reflections of Earth provide a fittingly spectacular climax.

▼ CityWalk

Universal Orlando does a better job than Disney at creating a relatively happening nightlife venue, which includes such hot spots as *Jimmy Buffet's Margaritaville*.

P.105 ▸ CITYWALK

▼ Cricketers Arms

This Orlando take on the friendly British pub is ideal for those who are homesick for televised soccer matches, fish'n'chips, and warm beer.

P.122 ▸ INTERNATIONAL DRIVE AND RESTAURANT ROW

▲ The Roxy

If hip-hop is your flavor, head directly to this nightclub to rub shoulders and hips with like-minded party people.

P.128 ▸ DOWNTOWN ORLANDO

▼ Adventurers Club

The best nocturnal diversion at Disney's Pleasure Island is not a nightclub, but a quirky and slightly surreal 1930's gentleman's club, with eclectic performances throughout the night.

P.86 ▸ DOWNTOWN DISNEY

▲ Illuminations: Reflections of Earth

Disney's original nighttime extravaganza still does a great job of lighting up the skies with fireworks and other effects.

P.65 ▸ EPCOT

▲ Downtown Orlando

Nowhere in Orlando – and arguably Central Florida – comes close to matching Downtown's supremely varied choice of bars, lounges, and clubs.

P.128 ▸ DOWNTOWN ORLANDO

Amusement rides

In addition to the predictable rollercoasters, there are a number of different styles of rides in the theme parks. Flight simulators are used with visual effects to take you on a journey to remote and exotic destinations. Ground- or water-based buggies travel sedately through lands populated by Audio-Animatronics robots in various human, animal, and extra-terrestrial forms. Or an entire adventure could take place as you sit and watch 3-D images pass before your bespectacled eyes.

▲ The Disney-MGM Studios Backlot Tour

A must-see for movie buffs interested in how films are made – and a reminder that Disney-MGM Studios is also a working production studio.

P.66 ▶ DISNEY-MGM STUDIOS

▲ The Amazing Adventures of Spider-Man

A strong candidate for Orlando's best all-round attraction, combining sensory effects, a touch of speed, and a popular theme to great effect.

P.95 ▶ ISLANDS OF ADVENTURE

▲ Back to the Future The Ride

The best flight-simulator ride of them all, where the great visuals divert your mind completely from the bumps, jerks, and anything likely to upset your stomach.

P.92 ▸ UNIVERSAL STUDIOS

▼ Kilimanjaro Safaris

This ride comes about as close as you can to re-creating an African safari, with the help of some of the continent's most recognizable animals and imaginative landscaping.

P.73 ▸ DISNEY'S ANIMAL KINGDOM

▲ Mickey's PhilharMagic

The latest 3-D attraction to grace Walt Disney World takes you on a truly magical journey with Daffy Duck and friends.

P.55 ▸ MAGIC KINGDOM

Gay Orlando

Orlando is a combination of the more liberal attitudes that prevail in southern Florida and the conservatism that characterizes the north of the state – that averages out to a relatively modest gay scene. A couple of nightclubs have established decent reputations, while Parliament House is a full-on gay resort; otherwise, there are more than enough gay-friendly establishments to go around.

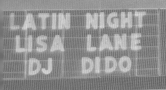

▲ Gay Day

Thousands of gays and lesbians visit en masse to rub shoulders with Mickey and Minnie during four very surreal days at Disney (and Universal).

P.175 ▶ ESSENTIALS

▲ The Courtyard at Lake Lucerne

Historic hotel with plenty of charm and character extends a warm welcome to gay visitors.

P.163 ▶ ACCOMMODATION

▶ Parliament House

Bars, drag queens, hotel rooms, and even a beach, all in one location, make this the equivalent of Orlando's gay theme-park.

P.163 ▶
ACCOMMODATION

▲ Pulse

Come to this hopping nightclub for its great sound system, special lighting effects, and some risqué live entertainment.

P.128 ▶ DOWNTOWN ORLANDO

▼ Southern Nights

A stylish renovation has brought Orlando's oldest and most famous gay and lesbian nightclub right up to date, providing a snazzy setting for spirited theme-nights.

P.128 ▶ DOWNTOWN ORLANDO

Gourmet restaurants

As an antidote to the all-you-can-eat buffets, chains, and themed dining experiences – not to mention all the sugary snack spots in the parks – you may well embrace a visit or two to some of Orlando's more renowned restaurants. The area has more than its share of extremely high-quality spots, both in terms of food and service. Primary locations for the top gourmet restaurants are Walt Disney World, International Drive, and downtown Orlando.

▲ Christini's Ristorante Italiano

You'll find Orlando's best Italian restaurant in an area on International Drive known as "Restaurant Row" by locals.

P.120 ▸ INTERNATIONAL DRIVE AND RESTAURANT ROW

▼ Ming Court

This superb Asian restaurant has gourmet fare for surprisingly low prices.

P.121 ▸ INTERNATIONAL DRIVE AND RESTAURANT ROW

▼ Victoria & Albert's

Dine on exquisite international cuisine at Central Florida's top-rated restaurant, located in Disney's *Grand Floridian Resort & Spa*. If you reserve well enough in advance, you can be attended to by the chef himself – a memorable experience.

P.82 ▶ THE REST OF WALT DISNEY WORLD

▼ Atlantis

This intimate restaurant specializes in fresh, simple, and delicious seafood dishes.

P.120 ▶ INTERNATIONAL DRIVE AND RESTAURANT ROW

▲ Jiko – The Cooking Place

Adding a welcome cosmopolitan flavor to Disney's collection of upscale eateries, this spot serves up spicy curries that you can wash down with excellent South African wines.

P.82 ▶ THE REST OF WALT DISNEY WORLD

▼ HUE – A Restaurant

This is one of downtown Orlando's new breed of ultra-trendy restaurants, where sipping a cocktail at the bar with the beautiful people is as much fun as dinner.

P.127 ▶ DOWNTOWN ORLANDO

Cooling off

Though Orlando isn't on the coast, there are still plenty of places to cool off – and you'll find that water is used in quite inventive ways to drench people. You can escape the summer heat at the water parks, both at Disney and elsewhere, splash about in the swimming pools that you'll find at almost every hotel, or zip down flume rides (water-based rollercoasters) where the fun is in the soaking that you're bound to get.

▲ Daytona Beach

It may be on the slightly tacky side, but this seaside town with a sandy beach is just a short hop – 50 miles – from Orlando.

▲ Wet 'n' Wild

Conveniently located on International Drive, this lively water park is packed with exciting rides for the whole family.

▶ Hotel swimming pools

The larger resort hotels, such as the *World Center Marriott Resort*, often boast multiple swimming pools in all shapes and sizes.

P.159 ▶ ACCOMMODATION

▶ Disney's water parks

Disney's two water parks, Blizzard Beach and Typhoon Lagoon, offer a welcome respite during the humid months.

P.78 ▶ THE REST OF WALT DISNEY WORLD

◀ Dudley Do-Right's Ripsaw Falls

You will get absolutely soaked on this flume ride, so you may want to bypass it on cooler days – unless you don't mind some teeth-chattering shivers before drying off.

P.97 ▶ ISLANDS OF ADVENTURE

◀ Swimming with dolphins

For many, simply being in the water next to these gentle and enigmatic creatures will trump any of Orlando's more elaborate entertainment options.

P.112 ▶ SEAWORLD ORLANDO AND DISCOVERY COVE

Museums and galleries

One of the main reasons for coming to downtown Orlando and its northern suburbs is to peruse the notable museums and galleries. Start with the paintings at the Orlando Museum of Art, drop into the Orlando Science Center if you have children to entertain, and then head up to a few more specialized collections in Winter Park and Maitland. You'll be pleasantly surprised to find so many worthy outlets of high culture in a city known more for mass consumerism.

▲ Albin Polasek Museum & Sculpture Gardens

Beautiful gardens provide the perfect backdrop for Czech sculptor Albin Polasek's liturgical, mythical, and classical sculptures.

P.131 ▸ WINTER PARK, EATONVILLE, AND MAITLAND

▼ Telephone Museum

The wonderful collection of vintage telephones celebrates the entrepreneurial genius of a Maitland grocer nearly one hundred years ago.

P.135 ▸ WINTER PARK, EATONVILLE, AND MAITLAND

▲ Orange County Regional History Center

Come here for a revealing glimpse of what Orlando looked like before the arrival of Disney – nothing like the city you see today.

P.125 ▶ DOWNTOWN ORLANDO

▲ Charles Hosmer Morse Museum of American Art

Louis Comfort Tiffany's spectacular Art Nouveau lamps and windows are the indisputable highlights here.

P.130 ▶ WINTER PARK, EATONVILLE, AND MAITLAND

▲ Orlando Science Center

The interactive, hands-on displays go some way toward making stuff like physics palatable for the kids, while everyone will enjoy the IMAX-style film.

P.125 ▶ DOWNTOWN ORLANDO

▼ Orlando Museum of Art

Orlando's dynamic little art museum presents American art from the nineteenth century to the present day.

P.125 ▶ DOWNTOWN ORLANDO

Kids' Orlando

Nowhere in the world caters to children as much as Orlando and its theme parks – and a great part of an adult's enjoyment is watching the wide-eyed excitement of their offspring as they clamber onto rides and hug Disney characters. Even away from the theme parks, the fun is pervasive at numerous other attractions, restaurants, and hotels, such as the *Nickelodeon Family Suites by Holiday Inn*, which have been conceived especially with kids in mind.

▲ Nickelodeon Family Suites by Holiday Inn

The hotel that any self-respecting youngster would want to stay at, where every amenity and service has been designed and thought up for juvenile pleasure.

P.159 ▸ ACCOMMODATION

▲ World's largest McDonald's

With its ever-popular burgers and fries and a host of video games and other amusements, this *McDonald's* is especially hard for kids to avoid.

P.121 ▸ INTERNATIONAL DRIVE AND RESTAURANT ROW

▶ The Making of Me

This extremely sensitive portrayal of pregnancy and childbirth is one of Disney's best educational attractions.

P.59 ▸ EPCOT

▼ Green Meadows Petting Farm

The perfect opportunity for the little ones to stroke, pat, pamper, ride (and even milk) a greater variety of animals than you'll find at any other petting zoo.

P.142 ▸ SOUTH OF ORLANDO

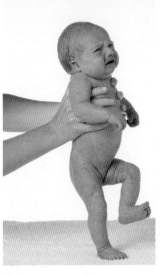

Shopping

Ignoring the tacky souvenir stalls, Orlando's shopping opportunities basically fall into two categories. There are the upmarket antique shops and art galleries found along Antique Row in downtown Orlando, Park Avenue in Winter Park, and the town of Mount Dora about forty miles from Orlando – good for browsing even if the price-tags will normally deter a purchase. And then there are the outlet shopping malls dotted all over town, where you'll have a hard time not buying the much-reduced name-brand clothes and such.

▲ Orlando Premium Outlets

You can do more than mere window-shopping for designer clothes at these factory outlet stores with knockdown prices.

P.119 ▶ INTERNATIONAL DRIVE AND RESTAURANT ROW

▲ World of Disney

The park's merchandising HQ, stocking a broad cross-section of the Disney souvenirs that you've seen elsewhere.

P.86 ▶ DOWNTOWN DISNEY

▲ Makinson Hardware Store

Check out the plastic models of horses and cattle that now fill Florida's oldest hardware store.

P.143 ▸ SOUTH OF ORLANDO

▼ Renningers Antique Center

Mount Dora is famous for its antique shops, many of which display their wares at this weekend market.

P.153 ▸ DAY-TRIPS

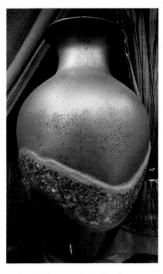

▲ Scott Laurent Galleries

One of the best art and gift galleries along Park Avenue, featuring some beautiful items that you might actually use.

P.136 ▸ WINTER PARK, EATONVILLE, AND MAITLAND

▼ Flea World

If you look hard enough, you might find the hidden gem that justifies the short drive from Orlando to this huge flea market.

P.152 ▸ DAY-TRIPS

Insider tips

Taking advantage of the numerous discounts, deals, and offers in Orlando, stands to save you plenty of time and money. Hidden beneath the masses of publicity hyping everything visitor-related to the nth degree, you'll find some very useful ways, from coupons to inexpensive trolley rides, to enhance your vacation experience and spend fewer dollars – if not totally beat the system.

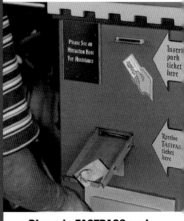

▲ Disney's FASTPASS and Universal Express

These two hugely successful systems employed at Disney and Universal are your best bet for avoiding mammoth waiting lines.

P.172 ▶ ESSENTIALS

▲ All-Star Resorts

Staying on Disney property was too expensive for most until these budget resorts opened.

P.159 ▶ ACCOMMODATION

▲ I-Ride Trolley

Frequent, cheap, and driven by the friendliest bus drivers on Earth, this is the most efficient way of traveling up and down International Drive.

`P.171` ▸ ESSENTIALS

▼ Discount coupons

Dismiss the coupons you see virtually everywhere at your peril, since the reductions they offer in restaurants, malls, hotels, and attractions really add up.

`P.170` ▸ ESSENTIALS

▶ Multi-park, multi-day tickets

Spreading your time at the major parks over several days is much more relaxing and saves you money on admission prices to boot.

`P.172` ▸ ESSENTIALS

Green Orlando

You don't have to travel too far out of Orlando to immerse yourself in nature. Lakes provide much of the fun – along with your best chances of spotting wildlife – while protected areas such as the Blue Spring State Park and The Disney Wilderness Preserve are excellent places to simply get away from it all. In the city itself, meanwhile, you'll find several attractive parks and gardens that afford a welcome break from the concrete and traffic.

▲ Harry P. Leu Gardens

The city's botanical gardens offer a visual and olfactory treat for plant and flower enthusiasts.

P.126 ▸ DOWNTOWN ORLANDO

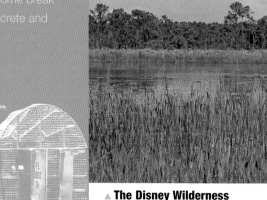

▲ The Disney Wilderness Preserve

To mitigate the environmental impact of their massive theme parks, Disney protects this peaceful 8500-acre patch of land where no construction will ever take place.

P.142 ▸ SOUTH OF ORLANDO

▶ Airboat ride on a Florida swamp

Feel the wind in your hair as you zip across a Florida lake, always on the lookout for alligators, bald eagles, and other local wildlife.

P.141 ▶ SOUTH OF ORLANDO

▼ Lake Eola

Right in the heart of downtown Orlando, this pretty lake and its surrounding park are prime spots for unwinding after work.

P.123 ▶ DOWNTOWN ORLANDO

▼ A World of Orchids

At this shop devoted to the lovely flowers, the pleasure is in the looking as much as the buying.

P.144 ▶ SOUTH OF ORLANDO

▲ Blue Spring State Park

Observe manatees in the wild at this attractive park boasting springs with year-round warm temperatures.

P.149 ▶ DAY-TRIPS

Show restaurants

If you really can't bear to stop the entertainment while you eat dinner, consider dining at one of Orlando's several show restaurants. The food is generally nothing to write home about, but it does come with a lively performance, ranging from large-scale extravaganzas with elaborate sets, costumes, and even horses, to more intimate affairs involving varying amounts of audience participation.

▲ Arabian Nights Dinner Show

The star performers are undoubtedly the beautiful horses, among them the Black Stallion, a gift from the creator of the eponymous fictional horse.

P.144 ▸ SOUTH OF ORLANDO

▲ Murderwatch Mystery Theatre

A small-scale production in which the audience is called upon to help solve a murder while stuffing their faces at the all-you-can-eat buffet.

P.86 ▸ DOWNTOWN DISNEY

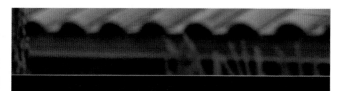

MAKAHIKI LUAU
POLYNESIAN FEAST & CELEBRATION

Aloha !

▲ Makahiki Luau Dinner Show

Come here for the costumes, music, and dance, which combine to create an enjoyable South Seas atmosphere.

P.113 ▸ SEAWORLD AND DISCOVERY COVE

◀ Medieval Times Dinner & Tournament

Be transported back to a time when knights jousted for the honor of a lady and the good townsfolk wolfed down spare ribs and Coke.

P.145 ▸ SOUTH OF ORLANDO

▼ Pirate's Dinner Adventure

A gigantic galleon is the setting for this adventure on the high seas, full of stunts and all the stereotypical pirate antics you could wish for.

P.121 ▸ INTERNATIONAL DRIVE AND RESTAURANT ROW

Orlando calendar

Beyond the theme parks, Orlando is one of Florida's most happening cities, with a calendar of festivals and events to match. The Florida Film Festival boasts a fine nationwide reputation, while the FUNAI Classic and Silver Spurs Rodeo attract a select field of professional golfers and cowboys, respectively.

▲ Florida Film Festival

Take a break from Hollywood blockbusters and sample a documentary, an animated film, or some Floridian cinema at this annual festival.

P.174 ▸ ESSENTIALS

▲ Daytona Bike Week

The most infamous yearly gathering of thousands of leather-clad bikers takes place in the nearby seaside resort of Daytona Beach.

P.174 ▸ ESSENTIALS

▲ Silver Spurs Rodeo

The fact that Kissimmee hosts the most important rodeo east of the Mississippi is testament to Central Florida's cattle-rearing past.

P.175 ▸ ESSENTIALS

▼ FUNAI Classic

Orlando's most famous resident, Tiger Woods, was a past winner of this professional tournament played on a Disney golf course.

P.175 ▸ ESSENTIALS

Offbeat Orlando

The quest of independent and adventurous tourists is to find an original idea in a city saturated with every fly-by-night attraction and trivial diversion imaginable. Fortunately, you'll discover several out-of-the-ordinary attractions in Orlando itself or just a short drive away. Nowhere is more off the beaten path than the spiritualists' village of Cassadaga, while Celebration, The Villages, and the Cypress Cove Nudist Resort & Spa are the havens of the rich, the old, and the naked respectively.

▼ The Villages

Understand why people choose to retire in Central Florida by staying at this sumptuous seniors community for a few nights.

P.147 ▶ DAY-TRIPS

▼ Cypress Cove Nudist Resort & Spa

Nudism is strongly encouraged at this resort – but be sure to support the wobbly bits when playing tennis and jogging, for example.

P.164 ▶ ACCOMMODATION

▼ Reptile World Serpentarium

Marvel as George VanHorn extracts venom from his collection of deadly snakes – no better proof that one man's pleasure is another man's poison.

P.140 ▶ SOUTH OF ORLANDO

▲ Celebration

Disney's idea of what the ideal American community should look and feel like is brought to life in this picture-perfect town where wholesome values reign.

P.138 ▶ SOUTH OF ORLANDO

▼ Gatorland

Orlando's oldest park continues to thrive amidst stiff competition by showcasing Florida's ever-fascinating alligators in a fun and friendly atmosphere.

P.138 ▶ SOUTH OF FLORIDA

▼ Cassadaga

The spiritualists who have made this village in the middle of a forest their home will gladly dispense advice and guidance if you cross their palms with silver.

P.148 ▶ DAY-TRIPS

Places

The Magic Kingdom

Opened in 1971, the Magic Kingdom has much in common with the original Disney theme park, Disneyland, built in California in 1955. Beyond the rides, shows, and costumed characters, the template is the same: a rose-colored vision of life coupled with an unrivaled attention to detail and a whole-hearted commitment to keeping visitors happy no matter what. The dramatic Cinderella Castle lies in the middle of it all, surrounded by seven themed sections: Main Street, USA; Adventureland; Frontierland; Liberty Square; Tomorrowland; Fantasyland; and Mickey's Toontown Fair. The latter two are very much for youngsters, bursting at the seams with Disney characters and tame rides, although the whole park emphasizes fantasy and family fun over thrills and spills. The attractions lying at the end of waiting lines that are frequently the longest in Disney will either make you look back nostalgically on your childhood or curse your gullibility, such is the variation in their quality. You'll also find a few edgier rides, notably Space Mountain and to a lesser extent Big Thunder Mountain Railroad, that provide a welcome change of pace.

Cinderella Castle

The most identifiable landmark in Disney World, a striking 189-foot pseudo-Rhineland palace with eighteen towers, is but an empty shell, housing much of the machinery required to run the rest of the park. A restaurant has recently opened in the structure itself, but otherwise there is little else to do inside the castle. At no time, however, is it more photogenic than during the spectacular fireworks display (see p.57) just before the park closes.

Jungle Cruise

Adventureland. Commentary by a pun-crazy guide is intended as half the fun of this slow boat ride down the Amazon, the Nile and the Mekong, where the Audio-Animatronics animals – from crocodiles to elephants, depending on which "river" you are navigating – look slightly less realistic in the cold light of day. The boats, accommodating twenty or so people, go at a pace

▼ JUNGLE CRUISE

For park hours and prices, see "Theme park practicalities" in Essentials.

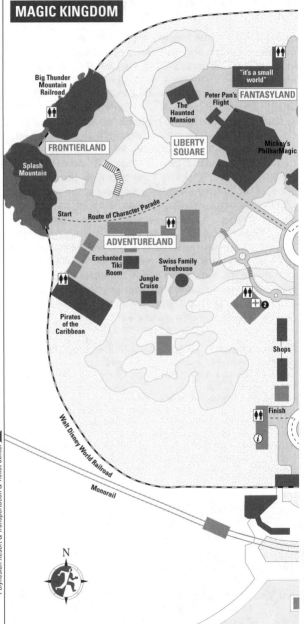

MAGIC KINGDOM

Big Thunder Mountain Railroad

"it's a small world"

Peter Pan's Flight

FANTASYLAND

The Haunted Mansion

FRONTIERLAND

LIBERTY SQUARE

Mickey's PhilharMagic

Splash Mountain

Start — Route of Character Parade

ADVENTURELAND

Enchanted Tiki Room

Swiss Family Treehouse

Jungle Cruise

2

Shops

Pirates of the Caribbean

Finish

Walt Disney World Railroad

Monorail

N

53

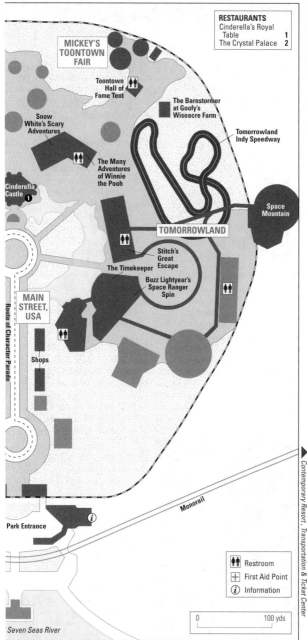

PLACES The Magic Kingdom

RESTAURANTS
Cinderella's Royal
 Table   1
The Crystal Palace   2

MICKEY'S
TOONTOWN
FAIR

Toontown Hall of
Fame Tent

The Barnstormer
at Goofy's
Wiseacre Farm

Snow White's Scary
Adventures

Tomorrowland
Indy Speedway

The Many
Adventures
of Winnie
the Pooh

Cinderella
Castle

Space
Mountain

TOMORROWLAND

Stitch's
Great
Escape

The Timekeeper

Buzz Lightyear's
Space Ranger
Spin

MAIN
STREET,
USA

Shops

Route of Character Parade

Contemporary Resort, Transportation & Ticket Center

Monorail

Park Entrance

Restroom
First Aid Point
Information

0   100 yds

Seven Seas River

Ferry to Transportation & Ticket Center

Saving time

Upon entering the park, don't be seduced by the appealing facades of old-fashioned town-square stores: they are all gift shops. Walk straight towards the Cinderella Castle and turn left – fewer people tend to tour the park in a clockwise direction, starting at Adventureland and working towards Tomorrowland. You can get a FASTPASS (see p.172) for the following attractions: Big Thunder Mountain Railroad, Buzz Lightyear's Space Ranger Spin, The Haunted Mansion, Jungle Cruise, The Many Adventures of Winnie the Pooh, Mickey's PhilharMagic, Peter Pan's Flight, Space Mountain, Splash Mountain, and Stitch's Great Escape.

gentle enough for the youngest visitors, and the occasional roars, screeches, and sprays of water provide the tiniest blips of excitment on what is generally a bland ride. The jokes, however, come so thick and fast that after a while they start to sound quite clever – another devious Disney mind-trick.

Pirates of the Caribbean

Adventureland. Disney's masterful laundering of X-rated themes such as drunkenness, sex, and violence is the great achievement of this boat ride around an island infested with pirates behaving very badly. As you pass burning buildings and dueling pirates you might expect your boat-buggy to make the occasional unexpected turn, but this sedate ride has no dicey moments.

▲ PIRATES OF THE CARIBBEAN

Splash Mountain

Frontierland. Minimum height: 40"/102cm. Like most flume rides, apart from a 52-foot drop guaranteed to get you wet, there are few scary moments. Enjoy this one, then, as much for cute Br'er Rabbit's adventures – depicted with Disney's exemplary attention to detail – as for its thrill factor. When not in freefall, the hollowed-out-log boats travel slowly enough for you to follow the storyline while building anticipation for the finale.

Big Thunder Mountain Railroad

Frontierland. Minimum height: 40"/102cm. A runaway train careers through a deserted mine in this venerable rollercoaster, still popular on account of its well-conceived theme and convincing setting in the heart of the Wild West, despite having become rather tepid in comparison with Orlando's newer thrill rides. On the other hand, most children will be able to handle this one.

The Haunted Mansion

Liberty Square. Board a Doom Buggy for a worthwhile, if not overly spooky, tour through a haunted house, populated by Audio-Animatronics vampires, gravediggers, and the like, who play a supporting role to ghosts and ghouls depicted by the impressive use of holograms. Since this is one of the park's longest rides, the sometimes lengthy waiting lines don't seem quite so bad.

Mickey's PhilharMagic

Fantasyland. Feast your eyes on brilliant 3-D imagery in this animated film set to classic Disney soundtracks, featuring Daffy Duck and other well-known characters. The effects, from 3-D kisses, popping champagne corks, and a memorable ride over the rooftops with Aladdin, are so enchanting that worn-out grown-ups will forget their tired feet and readily believe that carpets can fly.

▲ BIG THUNDER MOUNTAIN RAILROAD

Space Mountain

Tomorrowland. Minimum height: 44"/135cm. Originally the ride that everyone talked about after a visit to Disney World, this venerable rollercoaster has stood the test of time remarkably well, primarily because everything takes place in complete darkness. The twin tracks are set entirely inside a white, spiraling concrete colossus – besides the flashes of light from passing stars and meteors, you see nothing. This heightens the element of surprise, reinforcing the fear factor at every turn and plunge, even though the smallish cars don't travel at particulary fast speeds.

Stitch's Great Escape

Tomorrowland. Minimum height: 38"/95cm. The fearsome creature of The ExtraTERRORestrial Alien Encounter, the attraction's former name, has been replaced by the more kid-friendly Stitch, but the concept remains the same, with the mischievous monster escaping from a cage in the middle of a theater-in-the-round and wreaking havoc with such things as chilli dogs – which you can smell thanks to the impressive multi-sensory effects.

Orientation

The Magic Kingdom has a circular layout, with its seven distinct "lands" built around the famous Cinderella Castle icon. Upon entering the park, everyone has to walk up **Main Street, USA**, a nostalgic re-creation of a busy turn-of-the-century American shopping street, which leads to a junction just in front of the Cinderella Castle. Turning left at this junction and working your way around the park in a clockwise direction brings you first to **Adventureland**, with its jungle scenery and emphasis on exotic animals. **Frontierland** lies just to the north, inspired by the Wild West and dominated by the Big Thunder Mountain Railroad. Across a large lake (but accessible via a path from either Frontierland or Adventureland), **Liberty Square** is a relatively small area commemorating America's colonial heritage. Next comes the kid-oriented **Fantasyland**, where various fairytales are brought to life in rides and shows, and the multicolored **Mickey's Toontown Fair**, a whimsical village in which Mickey and Minnie Mouse are supposed to live. Finally, in the easternmost section of the park, **Tomorrowland** provides a glimpse into the future, with many of the attractions having something or other to do with outer space.

▲ SPACE MOUNTAIN

These effects, along with some of the best Audio-Animatronics to be found in Disney, are the attraction's strong point, but the ride offers relatively little in terms of thrill factor.

Other rides and attractions

Most of the rest of the park's rides and attractions will appeal to children much more than to adults. The park is starting to show its age in the kid-oriented Fantasyland; its spinning cups and saucers, flying elephants, and merry-go-rounds are the staple rides that you'd find in any village fairground. **Peter Pan's Flight**, **Snow White's Scary Adventures**, and **The Many Adventures of Winnie the Pooh** are all whimsical rides through these well-known fairytales – easily missed for anyone who has reached puberty, but very popular with the youngest visitors. Lengthy waiting lines also beckon at **"it's a small world"** which, if you can put up with the endless singing of the theme song, is a pleasant boat ride around a world of multiethnic dolls.

Adjoining Fantasyland, Mickey's Toontown Fair is the best place in the park to meet Disney characters; all the usual suspects are around throughout the day for autographs and handshakes in the **Toontown Hall of Fame Tent**, though

the only notable ride is **The Barnstormer at Goofy's Wiseacre Farm**, a relatively calm, kid-friendly rollercoaster.

The lines are always long at the **Tomorrowland Indie Speedway**, but this go-cart ride is disappointingly tame. The much-hyped **Buzz Lightyear's Space Ranger Spin** is like being inside a video game: you can spin your buggy and fire at all manner of baddies, but with no prior explanation of the rules, the excitement wanes quickly. The best of Tomorrowland's other attractions is **The Timekeeper** (unfortunately only open irregularly, on no set dates), a visually impressive journey through time using 360-degree images and offset by the wacky commentary of an Audio-Animatronics robot.

In Adventureland, the **Swiss Family Treehouse** is always worth a quick tour for its charming details; and **The Enchanted Tiki Room Under New Management** will at first have your toes tapping to the Broadway-style songs performed by Audio-Animatronics tropical birds, although the music soon becomes grating, and the same toes will start pointing towards the exit.

Shops

Main Street, USA

This entire stretch between the park entrance and Cinderella Castle is lined with gift shops, where you can buy everything from Mickey Mouse coffee and designer watches to, of course, those ubiquitous mouse-ear monogrammed caps. The shops offer a comphrehensive selection of the most sought-after merchandise, much of it overpriced and tacky but still an inevitable draw.

▲ WISHES FIREWORKS DISPLAY

Restaurants

Cinderella's Royal Table
Cinderella Castle. Cinderella and company are present as you wolf down decent prime rib, lamb shank, and other meaty dishes; lunch costs around $15, dinner $25. The grand dining room with its high ceilings and stained-glass windows is on the second floor of the castle. If you want to attend the very popular character breakfast (adults $21.99, children under 11 $11.99), be sure to reserve well in advance by calling ☎407/WDW-DINE.

The Crystal Palace
Off Main St. Hectic, brightly lit, turn-of-the-century-themed dining room, patrolled by Winnie the Pooh and friends, where the unspectacular but filling breakfast ($17.99), lunch ($18.99), and dinner ($22.99) buffets are kept fresh by chefs

▼ CINDERELLA'S ROYAL TABLE

constantly preparing new food, including BBQ chicken, carved ham, plenty of salads, and sticky desserts.

Live shows

Share a Dream Come True Parade
Daily 3pm, begins next to Splash Mountain, ends at park entrance. The kids will never forgive you if you miss Disney's signature character parade, headed by Micky Mouse in a giant snow globe leading a procession of characters from Disney's most beloved stories, including Pinocchio and the Evil Queen from Snow White. Standing near the departure point will save waiting time and allow you to get back to touring the park more quickly.

Wishes
Daily at park closing time, around Cinderella Castle. Of all the imaginative efforts to create an aura of fantasy, this simple but stunning twelve-minute fireworks display around the Castle is the most magical of them all. The display is set to a musical score of classic Disney songs. You can see the fireworks from anywhere in the park, though the best viewing points are facing the Cinderella Castle at the end of Main Street, USA.

EPCOT

The Experimental Prototype Community of Tomorrow, better known as EPCOT, opened in 1982, not as the real community engaging in cutting-edge experiments and developing new technologies that Walt Disney had envisaged when the idea took shape in the 1960s, but as a general celebration of human achievement. Covering an energy-sapping 300 acres, the park is divided into two areas. Future World consists of several pavilions vaunting mankind's progress in areas such as communications, agriculture, and science, with many of the exhibits striving to educate as much as entertain (which can sometimes bore the littler ones). The picturesque World Showcase, with its cultural film presentations, ethnic restaurants, and striking replicas of famous world landmarks built around a large lagoon, is the most extensive tribute to foreign cultures on offer in Orlando. Because of EPCOT's considerable size, the crowds are absorbed well and strolling about tends to be less stressful than at the other Disney parks.

Spaceship Earth

Spaceship Earth Pavilion. The story of how mankind has, does, and will in the future communicate with one another is told in the imposing geosphere that serves as EPCOT's signature landmark. Named for a phrase coined by its inventor, futurist Buckminster Fuller, the geodesic dome encompasses more space without internal supports than any other enclosure – and is perhaps the most eloquent realization of Fuller's "more for less" architectural dictum. Inside, a slow-moving buggy winds its way through the Ages of Man, brought to life by a diverse range of Audio-Animatronics characters, before making its final poignant ascent into the star-filled core of the geosphere.

Ellen's Energy Adventure

Universe of Energy Pavilion. Comedian Ellen de Generes tries her best to explain the world's energy sources in as nonscientific and fun a way as possible, but despite some good cinematography on enormous screens, there is only so much entertainment value in oil

▼ SPACESHIP EARTH

For park hours and prices, see "Theme park practicalities" in Essentials.

Saving time

Upon entering the park, the inclination of EPCOT first-timers is to check out what's going on in the golfball-like geosphere. Therefore, go instead directly to Mission: Space and Test Track, the two most popular rides, and obtain a FASTPASS for one and join the line (which should be short enough if you arrive early) for the other. You can get a FASTPASS for the following attractions: Honey, I Shrunk the Audience; Living with the Land; Maelstrom; Mission: Space; and Test Track.

pumps, coal mines, and natural gas plants. Dinosaurs, however tenuous their link in the energy chain, are much more fun, and a buggy-ride through a primeval forest inhabited by realistic Audio-Animatronics dinosaurs is the highlight.

Wonders of Life Pavilion

This pavilion is often closed (on no set dates and for reasons known only to Disney), which is a shame, since it contains some enjoyable attractions. **Cranium Command**, for instance, is an imaginative, humorous, and ultimately very entertaining theater show in which the audience helps to pilot the brain of a 12-year-old all-American boy, with actors speaking up for different parts of the kid's body. In **The Making of Me**, meanwhile, the dreaded "birds-and-the-bees" talk is made much easier by a touching film presentation

of conception, pregnancy (which includes actual footage of a developing fetus), and childbirth, one of the few educational attractions in the park that manages to strike a chord with children.

In the pavilion's other draw, **Body Wars** (minimum height: 40"/102cm), the idea is promising enough – a journey in a "body probe" through a human artery – but the flight-simulator technology used to realize it is somewhat dated. Be prepared for a bumpy ride as you make flying visits to the heart, lungs, and brain, and are attacked by white blood cells.

Mission: Space

Mission: SPACE Pavilion. Minimum height: 44"/112cm. The park's newest ride is a realistic attempt to turn you into an astronaut on a voyage to Mars. You are given one of four roles to play during the voyage

▼ MISSION: SPACE

EPCOT

EATING & DRINKING

Chefs de France/ Bistro de Paris	2
Le Cellier	4
Restaurant Akershus	3
Restaurant Marrakesh	1
San Angel Inn	5

♦♦ Restroom
✚ First Aid Point
ⓘ Information

WORLD SHOWCASE

Japan Pavilion
Morocco Pavilion
The American Adventure
U.S.A. Pavilion
Italy Pavilion
France Pavilion
La Signature
Germany Pavilion

N

World Showcase Lagoon

▶ EPCOT resort hotels

China Pavilion
Yong Feng Shangdian
Norway Pavilion
Maelstrom
The Puffin's Roost
Mexico Pavilion

United Kingdom Pavilion

FUTURE WORLD

Canada Pavilion

Honey, I Shrunk the Audience
Imagination! Pavilion

Test Track Pavilion

Ice Station Cool

The Land Pavilion

Mission: SPACE Pavilion

Innoventions East
Innoventions West

Living with the Land
The Circle of Life

Wonders of Life Pavilion

Universe of Energy Pavilion
Ellen's Energy Adventure
Park Entrance
Spaceship Earth Pavilion

The Living Seas Pavilion

Monorail Station

0   100 yds

▼ Transportation & Ticket Center

– pilot, navigator, engineer, or commander – which basically involves pushing a few buttons when prompted to do so. The capsule is compact and the computer-generated graphics that are played on a screen a few inches from your face are based on actual data from satellites that have orbited Mars.

The best moment of the ride, however, is the take-off, where cutting-edge flight-simulator technology creates real G-force – so not an activity to do just before or after lunch. The most effective way of reducing motion sickness is to keep focused on the screen in front of you.

Test Track

Test Track Pavilion. Minimum height: 40"/102cm. The park's only rollercoaster ride promises plenty of high-speed excitement, but delivers disappointingly little in the way of thrills and spills. It gets too bogged down by its high-performance-car-testing theme, which can seem overly technical for a thrill ride. You board your test vehicle and undergo a series of tests to see how the car performs in different situations. The net result is a mild-mannered sequence of bumps, jerks and jolts, and only the last thirty seconds or so, when the speed tests are carried out, are really exciting. On the plus side, this is one of the longest rides in Disney, lasting for more than five minutes.

Honey, I Shrunk the Audience

Imagination! Pavilion. This engaging 3-D presentation coordinates impressive visuals with low-tech "feelies"– which add sensations of touch and smell to the 3-D pictures – to give an audience "shrunk" by an inventor's Shrinking Gun plenty of amusing surprises, including being gently teased by white mice and a giant dog.

The Land

The Land Pavilion. The main attraction in The Land Pavilion, **Living with the Land** is an entertaining and informative fourteen-minute boat ride through several greenhouses showcasing farming techniques from around the world, from crop growing in the Tropics to fish farming. The focus on food production gives Disney researchers the opportunity to proudly display their Mickey Mouse–shaped cucumbers, watermelons, and pumpkins, while the ride's commentary touts the different kinds of fish served in the park's restaurants. In the pavilion's other attraction, the thought-provoking **The Circle of Life**, characters from *The Lion King* stress the need for protecting the environment through an amusing fable.

The Living Seas

The Living Seas Pavilion. The entire EPCOT geosphere

▲ THE LIVING SEAS

could fit into this massive saltwater aquarium, where a coral reef supports more than two thousand fish. The sharks, dolphins, turtles, rays, and multitude of tropical fish are best viewed at feeding times; or else you can fork out $140 to dive amongst them yourself (certified divers only; for reservations, call ☎407/939-8687). To get to the aquarium viewing area, which is spread over two floors, you have to descend in a "hydrolator," which lets you out at a mock undersea research facility, with exhibits and a film on marine exploration – all worth a brief glance once you have had enough of the fish.

Innoventions

Innoventions Pavilion. This pavilion is divided into two sections: Innoventions East is for the young and old; Innoventions West is geared primarily for

▼ SEGWAY AT INNOVENTIONS

the kids. Both are full of the latest in technological gadgetry, many of which you can fiddle and play with. You can, for example, design and build a plastic robot at East's Fantastic Plastics Works, or give your kids a crash course in fire safety at West's Where's the Fire? It must be said, however, that aside from the impressive Segways (electric vehicles operated by tilting one's body backward and forward and from side to side) driven around by the smug staff, the offerings are disappointingly mundane, and this part of the park merits only a cursory look.

Ice Station Cool

Next to Innoventions West.
Unmarked and undescribed on the park's official map, this Coca-Cola–sponsored tribute to liquid refreshments from around the world offers free samples of fizzy oddities like the surprisingly tasty Lychee Mello from Thailand, Smart Watermelon from China, Mozambican ginger beer, and other sugary drinks that ironically have been driven to the brink of extinction by the omnipotence of Coca-Cola.

World Showcase

Open from 11am. When EPCOT was in its developmental stages, eleven countries took up Disney's invitation to showcase their history, culture, architecture, and people; France built a replica Eiffel Tower in their pavilion, Mexico a Mayan pyramid, and the United Kingdom a pub, all around a forty-acre lagoon adjoining Future World. The eclectic collection of buildings with their waterfront setting form a picturesque ensemble

– this is by far the most attractive area of the park, albeit a slightly surreal one. People from the participating countries arrived to staff the restaurants and gift shops, adapting uneasily to the never-ending smiles and over-exuberance generally expected of Disney's "cast members." Indeed, the more low-key atmosphere of World Showcase is part of its appeal. You can also eat more exotically here than at any other theme park, and shop for things other than stuffed toys and mouse ears.

Be sure not to miss the excellent film presentations in the **Chinese** and **French pavilions**, giving a mouth-watering resume of these countries' treasures; they'll have you racing to the nearest travel agent. A similar film on Canada is also impressive, if a touch monotonous.

The most high-profile attraction takes place at the flagship **USA Pavilion**, where Audio-Animatronics versions of Benjamin Franklin and Mark Twain front a predictably patriotic 30-minute account of American history in The American Adventure, which describes the major events in this nation's 200-plus years using a combination of film footage and special effects. **Norway** tries to make the most of their Viking past in Maelstrom, one of the few rides as such in this section of EPCOT, but this bland boat-trip is only worth it if there is no line.

Boats cross the lagoon at regular intervals throughout the day, linking the entrance with the German and Moroccan pavilions.

▲ THE PUFFIN'S ROOST

Shops

La Signature

World Showcase, France. One of two locations in the world where you can find one-of-a-kind Guerlain fragrances, make-up, and the like.

The Puffin's Roost

World Showcase, Norway. Head past the pungent Norwegian perfume and plastic Viking helmets straight to the quality sweaters and Helly Hansen coats.

Yong Feng Shangdian

World Showcase, China. The most elaborate shop in the Disney theme parks catches the eye with its beautiful jade statues – but they also stock everything from porcelain dolls to fortune cookies.

Restaurants

Chefs de France/Bistro de Paris

World Showcase, France. Overseen by renowned French chefs Paul

▲ CHEFS DE FRANCE/BISTRO DE PARIS

Bocuse, Gaston Le Nôtre, and Roger Vergé, the food (some of which is flown in daily from France) and accompanying wine list are both top-notch. The authenticity of the cuisine, which includes foie gras, goat's cheese salad, *canard à l'orange*, and other French favorites, is not matched by the waiters, who are considerably more cheerful than their Parisian counterparts. Entrees at the less formal *Chefs de France* are around $25; at the *Bistro de Paris* upstairs they are $30 and up.

Le Cellier

World Showcase, Canada. While not one of the world's most identifiable cuisines, the Canadians do have tremendous cuts of beef, some decent ales and beers, and maple syrup – which features here in a salmon entree and the crème brûlée dessert. Well-prepared steaks ($20–30) dominate the menu.

Restaurant Akershus

World Showcase, Norway. The hearty all-you-can-eat $19.99 smorgasbord, which includes braised lamb and cabbage,

venison stew and herrings galore, is a good choice on colder days when the stomach requires a more substantial lining.

Restaurant Marrakesh

World Showcase, Morocco. The flavorful Moroccan menu includes *couscous* ($17.95) and *meshoui*, lamb roasted with vegetables ($23.95). Belly-dancers provide the entertainment.

San Angel Inn

World Showcase, Mexico. World Showcase's most atmospheric restaurant gives you the opportunity to eat under the stars on a balmy night in a picturesque Mexican village. It is often too dark to see what you are eating, which is a shame, since several dishes are more adventurous than the standard Tex-Mex fare, using ingredients such as cocoa and cactus. Lunch entrees $12–15; dinner around $20.

Live shows

Illuminations: Reflections of Earth

Daily at park closing time. EPCOT's

closing extravaganza takes place on World Showcase Lagoon, which, for thirteen breathtaking minutes, is made resplendent by fire, fireworks, and fountains, while video screens on a huge globe show moving images in keeping with the park's human achievement motif. Anywhere around the lagoon will provide a good vantage point, but if you want to be in the front rows, it's best to arrive about a half-hour early.

▲ SAN ANGEL INN

Disney-MGM Studios

After signing an agreement in the 1980s with Metro-Goldwyn-Mayer (MGM) to exploit the latter's many movie classics, Disney had an ample source of instantly recognizable images to mold into rides suitable for adults as much as for children. The resulting Disney-MGM Studios was opened in 1989, and of the four main Disney parks, it's the easiest to visit in a day. Too small to be divided into themed sections like the other parks, here the attractions – which include two excellent thrill rides, on a par with those at Universal's Islands of Adventure, and several entertaining live shows – lie along Hollywood-film-set-style streets sprouting off from a central square dominated by a giant replica of Mickey Mouse's sorcerer's hat from the film Fantasia. The park also doubles as a working production studio, churning out some of Disney's latest film offerings.

The Disney-MGM Studios Backlot Tour

Mickey Ave. The interest level of the 35-minute tour rises and falls, as you might expect from an attraction that, among many other things, visits the exterior shots of shows such as *The Golden Girls*. In addition to film and TV sets, you'll get a look at film props from *Star Wars* and other well-known movies, witness various special effects, and observe as people beaver away on new costumes and scenery at

For park hours and prices, see "Theme park practicalities" in Essentials.

this working production studio. The best moment comes at the end when you arrive at the Catastrophe Canyon movie set to witness pyrotechnics and other great effects at disturbingly close range. The tour is kept relevant by the regular addition of props from recent MGM and Disney movies.

▼ SAN FRANCISCO FILM SET

Saving time

There is a notice board in the center of the park giving regularly updated waiting times for every attraction. You can get a FASTPASS for the following attractions: Indiana Jones Epic Stunt Spectacular, Rock 'n' Roller Coaster, Star Tours, The Twilight Zone Tower of Terror, and Voyage of The Little Mermaid.

Who Wants to Be a Millionaire – Play It!

Mickey Ave. Make a special effort to attend this mock filming of the well-known quiz show, done with admirable accuracy in a real TV studio. Anyone in the audience can earn the right to advance to the "hot seat" by answering a general question quicker than the rest, and once there they will be playing for a top prize of a three-day Disney Line cruise (see p.173) for four people, including airfare. (Go to Guest Relations at the park entrance for details of the rules and regulations of this game.) Places are limited, so arrive a bit in advance of published show times.

Walt Disney: One Man's Dream

Mickey Ave. A somewhat understated attraction which, through museum-style exhibits and a 25-minute documentary film, gives a surprisingly sober account – free from the self-adulation that you might have expected – of how this son of a Missouri farmer made good.

The Great Movie Ride

Mickey Ave. Movie buffs will enjoy this nostalgic ride through scenes from several classic films, from *Public Enemy*'s Gangster Alley to *The Wizard of Oz*'s Yellow Brick Road. The attraction is given a welcome additional dimension by real-life actors who interact with the Audio-Animatronics movie stars. Although both humans and robots give equally cheesy performances, they combine well enough – re-enacting favorite movie moments with a generous dose of slapstick comedy – to hold the audience's attention.

Rock 'n' Roller Coaster

Off Sunset Blvd. Minimum height: 48"/122cm. Board your VIP limousine for a high-speed trip to an Aerosmith concert. The band's high-energy music accompanies you throughout this thrilling ride and, like it or not, certainly helps keep the adrenaline pumping. The rollercoaster starts at break-neck speed and maintains an exhilarating pace through several loop-the-loops, all done in complete darkness.

The Twilight Zone Tower of Terror

End of Sunset Blvd. Minimum height: 40"/102cm. The well-conceived theme is half the fun of this thrill ride in which a mysterious service elevator in the creepy thirteen-story Hollywood

▼ THE GREAT MOVIE RIDE

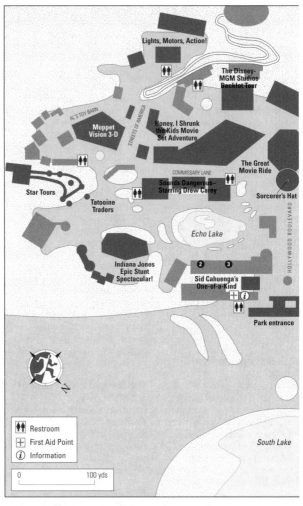

Lights, Motors, Action!

The Disney-MGM Studios Backlot Tour

AL'S TOY BARN

Muppet Vision 3-D

STREETS OF AMERICA

Honey, I Shrunk the Kids Movie Set Adventure

The Great Movie Ride

COMMISSARY LANE

Sounds Dangerous– Starring Drew Carey

Sorcerer's Hat

Star Tours

Tatooine Traders

Echo Lake

HOLLYWOOD BOULEVARD

Indiana Jones Epic Stunt Spectacular!

2 3

Sid Cahuenga's One-of-a-Kind

Park entrance

Restroom

First Aid Point

(i) **Information**

0   100 yds

South Lake

▲ THE TWILIGHT ZONE TOWER OF TERROR

Tower Hotel goes directly to the Twilight Zone. Upon boarding the elevator you're strapped into your seats and, instead of moving up or down, get wheeled past holograms depicting various ghostly apparitions, blasts of cold air, and

DISNEY-MGM STUDIOS

EATING & DRINKING	
50s Prime Time Café	2
Hollywood Brown Derby	1
Tune-In Lounge	3

Who Wants to be
a Millionaire–Play It!

Walt Disney:
One Man's Dream

MICKEY AVENUE

Voyage of The
Little Mermaid

Playhouse
Disney–
Live on Stage

ANIMATION
COURTYARD

The Magic of
Disney Animation

Rock 'n'
Roller Coaster

Attraction Waiting
Times information
board

SUNSET BOULEVARD

The Twilight Zone
Tower of Terror

Beauty & the Beast–
Live on Stage

Fantasmic!

Boats to
Disney Resorts

plenty of sinister music. When your journey through The Fifth Dimension begins in earnest, you'll experience several sudden drops – including moments of weightlessness – on one of four, randomly selected sequences, so no matter how many times you ride this one, you'll never quite know what's coming next.

Star Tours

End of Streets of America. Minimum height: 40"/102cm. The screen on this *Star Wars*–based flight simulator ride to the Moon of Endor is too small and far away from where you are sitting to fully convince you that your StarSpeeder is weaving its way through an asteroid storm and engaging in space battles. In the

▲ 50'S PRIME TIME CAFÉ

end, your attention is seldom diverted from the fact that you are being bumped around in a box, and all the ride really succeeds in doing is to prove that public transportation in outer space is no less nauseating than its equivalent in this world.

Muppet Vision 3-D

Streets of America. The humor of The Muppets – which here will appeal as much to adults as to children – and some fine 3-D effects, such as those accompanying Miss Piggy's song and Sam the Eagle's fireworks display, combine to make this one of the park's most entertaining attractions. The show takes place in a theater, complete with Audio-Animatronics versions of Statler and Waldorf, the two old hecklers cracking cheesy jokes from their box, and is full of the chaotic comedy that one would expect from Kermit and company.

Other rides and attractions

Both **Honey, I Shrunk the Kids Movie Set Adventure** and **Playhouse Disney – Live on Stage!** are strictly for the kids, with grown-ups relegated to sitting on the floor while their offspring clamber around a giant forest playground in the former attraction, or jig up and down with hyperactive Disney characters in the latter. **The Magic of Disney Animation** teaches you how to draw cute mice and ducks, and so will also appeal to children, while the short talk beforehand, in which the lecturer interacts cleverly with an animated version of Mushu, the small dragon from *Mulan*, gives an interesting insight into how a Disney character is thought up in the first place. Finally, **Sounds Dangerous – Starring Drew Carey** relies on sound effects, marred somewhat by poor-quality earphones, to tell a slapstick detective story.

Shops

Sid Cahuenga's One-of-a-Kind

Just after the park entrance. Specializing in movie posters and one-of-a-kind signed photos of stars from the big and small screens at not-so-kind prices.

Tatooine Traders

As you leave Star Tours. Fans of the *Star Wars* films will enjoy browsing through the memorabilia, which includes a $599 Limited Edition Lightsabre.

Restaurants

50's Prime Time Café

Opposite Echo Lake. Based on a kitchen in a 1950s all-American home, with plenty of communal tables but very few tables-for-two, this hectic restaurant is the ideal place to fill your kids up on decent meatloaf, fried chicken, and other comfort food, for around $13.

Hollywood Brown Derby

Opposite the sorcerer's hat. The large, softly lit, carpeted dining room sets a refined tone, where, despite the hordes of strollers parked outside, you can eat the park's best lunches ($15–20) and dinners ($20–28) in relative peace and quiet. The menu features excellent lamb, beef, salmon, and tuna, with a few salad options at lunch.

Bars

Tune-In Lounge

Opposite Echo Lake. Adjoining the *50's Prime Time Café*, this is one of the very rare bars in the Disney theme parks where you can buy alcohol. It is invariably packed, so you'll have to fight to get one of the several comfy chairs that fill the bar.

Live shows

Indiana Jones Epic Stunt Spectacular!

Next to Echo Lake. This grand presentation of scenes from the Indiana Jones movies is one of the best live shows at Disney. The stunts, which include plenty of fist-fighting, jumping from high buildings, and exploding vehicles, are performed by

trained professionals, while some audience participation provides just the right amount of humor. The climax of the show is a realistic and enthralling showdown between Indy and the bad guys on a moving airplane.

Beauty and the Beast – Live on Stage

Sunset Blvd. This abridged stage version of the famous love story has some reasonable acting (for Disney shows, that is), slick choreography, and superb costumes and sets.

Voyage of The Little Mermaid

Animation Courtyard. Colorful costumes and good sets are not quite sufficient to make the live performance of this nautical fairytale convincing. The addition of clips from the film and sensory effects such as salty air, mist, and wind help only a little.

Fantasmic

Daily at park closing time. Off Sunset Blvd. This dramatic show featuring lasers, lights, and a few fireworks thrown in for good measure takes place in Mickey's dreams, which provide sufficient license for the appearance of just about every Disney character ever created.

▼ INDIANA JONES EPIC STUNT SPECTACULAR!

Disney's Animal Kingdom

Disney's largest theme park, covering more than five hundred acres, is in many ways their greatest achievement to date. Florida's swampland has been transformed miraculously into the Asia and Africa of your most fanciful dreams, and at no point while touring the park do you ever feel like you're in a zoo – which is essentially what this is. The park is divided into six "lands," five of which are arranged around The Tree of Life, the signature landmark that rises over the first "land," Discovery Island, which sits in the center of the park and is linked to the other lands by bridges. Working in a clockwise direction around Discovery Island: Camp Minnie-Mickey resembles a summer camp in the Adirondacks; Africa and Asia are fabulous re-creations of the natural landscapes of these continents; Rafiki's Planet Watch educates visitors in nature conservation; and DinoLand USA is dedicated to dinosaurs.

Oasis and The Tree of Life

Upon entering the park all visitors pass through the Oasis, a verdant tropical garden inhabited by flamingos and other exotic animals, before crossing a bridge to Discovery Island. Here you'll find the park's superbly devised icon, The Tree of Life, a 145-foot concrete tree whose trunk and branches have been skillfully engraved with 325 cleverly intertwined images of all kinds of animals; look for the tortoises and kangaroos carved onto the tree's base.

It's Tough to be a Bug!

The Tree of Life. Deep down in the root system of The Tree of Life a multitude of bugs are waiting to put you in their shoes during this enjoyable 3-D show. The audience of "honorary bugs" is shown a demonstration that reveals the survival techniques of various creepy-crawlies, who manage to escape poisonous darts, acidic sprays, and

▼ FLAMINGOS IN ANIMAL KINGDOM

For park hours and prices, see "Theme park practicalities" in Essentials.

Saving time

Obtain a FASTPASS for Kilimanjaro Safaris, by far the park's biggest draw. You can get a FASTPASS for the following attractions: DINOSAUR, It's Tough to be a Bug!, Kali River Rapids, Kilimanjaro Safaris, and Primeval Whirl.

foul-smelling gases before a malevolant grasshopper attempts to exterminate the audience by way of giant fly-swatters and cans of "Bug Doom" insect spray, all brought to life by diverse "feelies" and captivating 3-D visuals. Children with a fear of "things that creep and crawl in the dark" should probably bypass this one.

Kilimanjaro Safaris

Africa. In this very successful attempt to re-create a real safari through the African savannah, giraffes, elephants, hippos, and rhinos all roam free; you'll also catch a glimpse of lions, though they tend to spend most of the daytime hours asleep. The tour is conducted in a large Jeep with commentary from the driver, who points out the animals while at the same time helping other park rangers track down make-believe poachers – an entertaining subplot that doesn't distract at all from your wildlife observation. The Jeep traverses the savannah at a steady pace, maximizing your chances of getting a good look at the animals and making photography easier, although all viewings are from a great enough distance to make a decent zoom lens worth having.

Pangani Forest Exploration Trail

Africa. Playful gorillas are the star attraction on this pleasant nature trail showcasing African wildlife, where you'll see animals that differ slightly from the normal zoo contingent, such as the Colobus monkey with its long bushy white tail and the giraffe-like okapi. You can observe most of the animals relatively up-close from the trail that winds through lush, jungle-like vegetation. Your first enounter with the gorillas is through a glass screen, but a little further on, as you cross the suspension bridge, you're rewarded with a better, open-air view of them. Another good photo opportunity comes at the hippo pool, where you may be surprised by how gracefully these creatures move underwater.

Rafiki's Planet Watch

East of Africa and north of Asia. Accessible only by taking the **Wildlife Express Train** from Africa – a 10-minute ride that passes the park's animal care facilities – this is the most openly educational section of the park. In **Conservation Station**, interactive exhibits promote nature conservation – although the constant reminders

▼ GORILLAS IN PANGANI FOREST EXPLORATION TRAIL

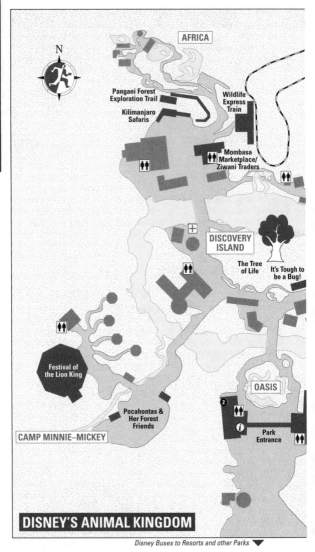

DISNEY'S ANIMAL KINGDOM

Disney Buses to Resorts and other Parks ▼

of what a good job Disney is doing in this respect verge on overkill. Be sure not to miss the simple yet incredibly touching **Song of the Rainforest**, where the sounds of the rainforest – from screeching birds to buzzing chainsaws – come alive as you sit with earphones in a darkened booth. Kids, meanwhile, will enjoy the opportunity to stroke sheep and goats at the adjacent **Affection Section** petting zoo.

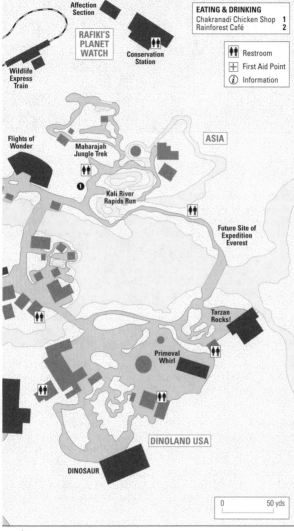

Kali River Rapids Run

Asia. Minimum height: 38"/97cm. The emphasis is very much on getting wet as you board a twelve-person raft for a swirling trip down the Chakrandi River. As with most water-based rides at Disney, the saturation far outweighs the excitement – except for young kids, for whom the saturation *is* the excitement. Since the raft spins in all directions during the ride, there is no particular position

▲ DINOSAUR

on board that will keep you drier than anywhere else.

Maharajah Jungle Trek

Asia. Although still good for a wander, the Asian-animal equivalent of Africa's Pangani Forest Exploration Trail is slightly less interesting than its counterpart, mainly because most of the animals aren't particularly active in front of crowds. The magnificent tigers, the trail's outstanding feature, lounge around the ruins of an ancient palace, looking very serene and well fed, while the Komodo dragons and fruit bats almost never move at all. You do at least get relatively up-close views of the wildlife.

DINOSAUR

DinoLand USA. More exciting than the usually tranquil journeys through Disney's Audio-Animatronics landscapes, this enjoyable ride on a twelve-seat "Time Rover" transports you back 65 million years with

▼ RAINFOREST CAFÉ

a mission to save a friendly iguanadon from extinction. You'll experience plenty of short drops and sudden stops in the dark as beasts spring menacingly from the prehistoric forest, roaring all the while. Air and smoke cannons, strobes, and other special effects help to further enhance the sense of danger.

Other rides and attractions

Both Africa and Asia have been constructed with great attention to detail, and strolling around them is a pleasure in itself. Opening in Asia in 2006 is a new, eye-catching thrill ride, **Expedition Everest**, based on the legend of the yeti and consisting of a rollercoaster ride on a nearly 200-foot mountain railway bound for the foot of Mount Everest. While in Africa, look out for the extremely talented musicians, dancers, and acrobats who perform at regular intervals throughout the day at various locations.

DinoLand USA is really little more than a fairground, where the only animals present are of the stuffed variety – which you can win in various fairground-style games – or Audio-Animatronics. Dominating this corner of the park are the twisting tracks of **Primeval Whirl**, a low-speed rollercoaster that tries to make up for its sluggishness by spinning buggies that make you want to puke.

Camp Minnie–Mickey features several live shows and plenty of Disney characters signing autographs.

Shops

Mombasa Marketplace/ Ziwani Traders

Africa. A small section of this shop sells authentic African crafts such as wooden statues, jewelry, and musical instruments – all infinitely more interesting than the rest of the stock, which consists of the usual Disney merchandise.

Restaurants

Rainforest Café

At the park entrance ☏407/938-9100, ⊛www.rainforestcafe.com. One of two Orlando locations (the other is in the Downtown Disney Marketplace ☏407/827-8500) of this safari-themed restaurant, where the interior jungle decor is more promising than the rather mediocre menu of pizzas, pasta dishes, and steaks. Prices for entrees range from $15 to $20.

Chakranadi Chicken Shop

Asia. This is the only park eatery serving even vaguely ethnic cuisine, in the form of small portions of stir-fry chicken for around $6, as well as some refreshing chai, or spiced milk, tea.

Live shows

Flights of Wonder

Asia. Watch in awe as some

▲ FESTIVAL OF THE LION KING

of the world's most beautiful birds, including owls and falcons, swoop over – and even interact with – the audience in the park's most charming live show.

Tarzan Rocks!

DinoLand U.S.A. A high-energy extravaganza in which singers bellow out rock songs amid the general chaos created by all-swinging, all-skating gymnast-actors.

Festival of The Lion King

Camp Minnie-Mickey. It helps if you like *The Lion King* soundtrack for this one, which is played ad nauseam as a huge cast of singers, dancers, acrobats, and characters from the movie put on a visually captivating Broadway-style show.

Pocahontas and Her Forest Friends

Camp Minnie-Mickey. Very much the show for young children, this small-scale production based on the Disney movie *Pocahontas* consists of little more than a girl prattling to a tree, cameo appearances by a few cute live animals, and a song.

The rest of Walt Disney World

Beyond the four main theme parks, the rest of Walt Disney World is a mixed bag: some sections every bit the equal of the biggies, while others are barely of passing interest – but all of it tries hard to keep you on Disney grounds and part you from your hard-earned dollar. Many of the attractions do at least offer a refreshing departure from the amusement-park concept in that they are intended for adults rather than children. Two excellent water parks provide welcome relief on hot days, and unique diversions such as stock-car driving and behind-the-scenes tours of several of Disney's main parks don't have analogs anywhere else. Sprinkled throughout are Disney's resort hotels (see Accommodation), which, in addition to offering some decent dining options, serve as mini-theme parks in themselves, each occupying its own landscaped plot, usually with several swimming pools and a beach beside an artificial lake, and based on some dreamy vacation theme.

Blizzard Beach

Near Disney-MGM Studios and All-Star Resorts ☏407/560-3400. Daily 9am–6pm or later in summer, 10am–6pm in winter. Adults $34, children 3–9 $28. Opened in 1995, this water park is meant to resemble a ski resort built in Florida after a freak snowstorm and now melting away under the sun. The theme may smack a little of desperation, but this does not detract from Blizzard Beach's visceral appeal. Those fond of thrill rides will head straight to the top of the snow-covered "mountain" that overlooks the park (taking the stairs rather than the busy chairlift is much quicker) to experience **Summit Plummet**, a terrifyingly steep 120-foot drop in the guise of

▲ WALT DISNEY WORLD ENTRANCE

a ski jump – the tallest and fastest water slide in the US and the most exhilarating ten seconds in Orlando. The other rides are tamer in comparison, but still good fun. The **Slush Gusher** speed-slide runs parallel to Summit Plummet, but at a less intimidating angle, while at the two-lane **Downhill Double Dipper** you can race against someone down a 200-foot water slide.

▲ TYPHOON LAGOON

Once exhausted, take time to relax in the calm wave-pool at Melt-Away Bay and sunbathe on the sandy beach that surrounds it. However, arrive early to secure a deck chair – on hot, sunny days you should ideally be there when the gates open.

Typhoon Lagoon

Just south of Downtown Disney
☏ 407/560-4141. Daily 10am–6pm in winter, 9am–6pm or later in summer. Adults $34, children 3–9 $28. The rides here are less intimidating than at Blizzard Beach, though still edgy enough to justify the cost of admission, and the tropical-island theme lends itself well to more sedate and relaxing activities, making this park a good choice for families with younger children. You can snorkel with benign sharks and pretty tropical fish in the saltwater **Shark Reef** or be swept gently along by the six-foot waves generated in the gigantic **Surf Pool** around which the park's other rides are built. Of these other rides, **Humunga Kowabunga**, a speed-slide where you have a choice of three different ways down, is the most exciting. In the park's newest ride, **Crush 'n' Gusher**, powerful jets of water propel you and your raft through several twists and turns, creating up-and-down movements vaguely like those on a rollercoaster. Unlike at the major parks, visitors can bring their own food (but no alcohol or glass containers) into Typhoon Lagoon; the Surf Pool's large sandy beach, which is crammed with deckchairs, is the obvious place for a picnic.

Disney's Wide World of Sports

Two miles east of Disney's Animal Kingdom on Osceola Parkway
☏ 407/939-GAME, ⊛ www .disneyworldsports.com. Hours depend on daily events. Adults $10.75, children 3–9 $8. The most recent extension to Disney World opened in 1997 and, despite its name, is not a theme park based on sports. Instead, it is a 200-acre complex of stadiums, arenas, and sports fields bustling on any given day with soccer moms, high-school wrestling teams, or pro baseball players. There is a small section called **The Sports Experience** where you can ascertain your baseball pitching speed – you

▲ BASKETBALL AT DISNEY'S WIDE WORLD OF SPORTS

may be surprised to find just how much slower you throw than the major leaguers – kick a field goal and test various other sporting skills, but this feels more like a fun diversion for competing athletes than an attraction for visitors. It's only really worth a special trip if you time it to coincide with a particular sporting event. The most publicized of these are the games played by the **Atlanta Braves** during March spring training, which take place in the 9500-seat baseball stadium (tickets $13–21). A full schedule of sporting events, both professional and amateur, is available on the website.

Richard Petty Driving Experience

Walt Disney World Speedway, at the south end of the Magic Kingdom parking lot ☎ 1-800/237-3889, ⊕ www.1800bepetty.com. Daily 9am–4pm, sporadic closures during Oct, Nov, and Dec. Although expensive, this attraction offers the ultimate payback for the NASCAR dad who has patiently walked his kids all over the Magic Kingdom.

Here you can board your very own NASCAR-style stock-car, either on your own or as a passenger, and ride it around a one-mile tri-oval track. The "Ride-Along" ($99) is the most basic of the several experiences offered: three laps of the track driven by an expert, reaching speeds of up to 150mph. If you want to take the wheel yourself – a much more daring but still safe enough choice – you can choose the intensive three-hour "Rookie Experience" ($379), at the end of which you drive eight laps; or the "King's Experience" ($749) and the "Experience of a Lifetime" ($1249), longer variations whereby you get to drive eighteen and thirty laps respectively. In all cases, you must be over 18 and have a valid driving license. If you're going to be driving, arrive thirty minutes in advance so that you can sign a liability waiver and be assigned a driving suit. The "Ride-Along" is available daily; the other experiences are offered daily except for Tuesday and Thursday.

Disney Institute

Buena Vista Drive, north of Downtown Disney ☎321/939-4600, ⊛www .disneyinstitute.com. The Disney Institute, modeled on a university campus done in Florida-style architecture, offers various business-related courses to anyone who wants to learn the techniques and practices that have made Disney so financially successful over the years. The interest for visitors, however, is in the tours run by the Institute giving a behind-the-scenes look at many aspects of Walt Disney World. The best – and most expensive at $199 (including lunch) – is the "Backstage Magic" tour, which takes you along the tunnel system beneath the Magic Kingdom and offers a look at some of the backstage goings-on at EPCOT and Disney-MGM Studios, including the technology required to put on a show such as The American Adventure (see p.63) and a peek at the elaborate costumes inside the Disney wardrobe. The tour lasts about seven hours and you must be over 16, not to mention rather dedicated to gaining a greater inside perspective on the parks – it's probably of less interest to first-time visitors trying to bag as many rides as possible.

Restaurants

Artist Point

Wilderness Lodge ☎407/939-3463. Hearty cuisine from the Pacific Northwest – salmon, halibut, and buffalo – is complemented by wines from the states of Washington and Oregon at this upscale restaurant with high wood-beamed ceilings. Main dishes are in the $20–30 range.

California Grill

Contemporary Resort ☎407/939-3463. Panoramic views over the Magic Kingdom, an unpretentious dining room, fresh sushi and fish dishes, an ever-changing choice of vegetarian meals, and an extensive selection of (sometimes rare) Californian wines makes this one of Disney's best all-round restaurants. Most entrees are $25–35; vegetarian dishes are less.

Everything Pop Shopping and Dining

Pop Century Resort ☎407/939-3463. The food court at this resort features the usual burgers (including a veggie burger option), hot dogs, and pizzas, along with other tempting (if not any healthier) recipes such as peanut butter fluff sandwiches ($4), buttermilk fried chicken ($9), and sloppy joes ($6).

▼ FLYING FISH CAFÉ

Flying Fish Café

BoardWalk Inn ☎407/939-3463.
Excellent fish, veal, and steak
are creatively prepared with
seasonal ingredients and served
in one of Disney's hippest
dining rooms, full of brightly-
hued fish motifs. The drawback
is the cost: most dinner entrees
are well over $30.

Jiko – The Cooking Place

Animal Kingdom Lodge ☎407/939-
3463. Enjoy typical American
fare such as steaks and ribs
with a welcome cosmopolitan
flavor of curried sauces and
exotic grains and spices, all
washed down with no less
than 65 different choices of
exclusively South African
wine. Dinner entrees typically
cost $25–30.

Victoria & Albert's

Grand Floridian Resort & Spa
☎407/939-3463. Central Florida's
top-rated restaurant offers
excellent cuisine and service.
The $95 (add another $50 or so
for wine), seven-course menu
is an extravagant treat which
changes slightly from day to day,
but always includes luxurious
starters such as foie gras or
caviar, and gourmet main dishes
prepared with great attention to
presentation. If you want to sit at
the Chef's Table in the kitchen,
where the chef himself attends to
your every whim, you'll have to
reserve months in advance.

Downtown Disney

If Disney World were a small American town, Downtown Disney would be its shopping mall. Bordered by a lake on one side and the Interstate (I-4) on the other, its three distinct areas – West Side, Pleasure Island, and Marketplace – are full of shops and restaurants that are more varied and interesting than those on offer at the theme parks, but still not overly original in the scheme of things. You'll also find a multi-screen cinema, a high-profile Cirque du Soleil show, and the video-game wonderland of DisneyQuest, along with several clubs and discotheques for adults only. It is free to enter Downtown Disney and stroll around; if you want to sample the nightlife, however, there is a charge.

West Side

Occupying roughly the western third of Downtown Disney, the emphasis in this area is on music and entertainment, though a few decent eating spots exist too. The biggest names to be found include the renowned Cirque du Soleil, which has a permanent base here, an outlet of the *House of Blues* chain, and a Virgin Megastore.

DisneyQuest

West Side. Sun–Thurs 11.30am–11pm, Fri–Sat 11.30am–midnight. Adults $34, children 3–9 $28. Spread rather claustrophobically over five floors are an assortment of virtual-reality games, some of which work very well indeed, others so pointless that their creators should take a virtual-reality check themselves. The better games are based loosely on rides at the Disney parks. **Virtual Jungle Cruise**, for example, puts you on a bumpy raft-ride through digital rapids, while **Cyber-Space Mountain** lets you design your own rollercoaster, then experience it in a flight simulator. Less fulfilling is **Buzz Lightyear's AstroBlaster**, a high-tech bumper-car ride with

▼ VIRTUAL JUNGLE CRUISE

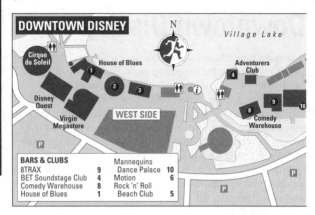

DOWNTOWN DISNEY

Village Lake

Cirque du Soleil

House of Blues

Adventurers Club

Disney Quest

WEST SIDE

Virgin Megastore

Comedy Warehouse

BARS & CLUBS			
8TRAX	9	Mannequins Dance Palace	10
BET Soundstage Club	4	Motion	6
Comedy Warehouse	8	Rock 'n' Roll	
House of Blues	1	Beach Club	5

asteroid-firing cannons that is as confusing as the real-life version in the Magic Kingdom. Of the new-generation video games, **Ride the Comix** is one of the best. You look a bit silly manipulating the controls, but this is quickly forgotten in the heat of a very realistic 3-D battle with an assortment of comic-book villains.

Once you get bored of sampling the video-game technology of today, you can play the classic games of yesteryear, such as Pac-Man, Space Invaders, and Donkey Kong, on the third and fifth floors.

Pleasure Island
☎407/939-1289. Free between 10am and 7pm, $20.95 after 7pm

gives access to all nightclubs, or $9.95 for access to one club. You must be at least 18 to enter the clubs and 21 to buy alcohol. A six-acre island in the middle of Downtown Disney, full of pseudo-warehouses and made to look as though it has been abandoned, represents Disney's attempt to provide some adult entertainment. Its faux-ghetto style would have made a handsome red-light district, but Disney has instead opted to fill Pleasure Island with a bunch of nightclubs that are as middle-of-the-road as one would expect; in truth, there are many more interesting nightlife options elsewhere, notably in downtown Orlando. For those staying on Disney property, however, Pleasure Island is very convenient, as buses link Downtown Disney to all of the Disney resorts and are timed to run until a little after the clubs close at 2am. Downtown Orlando, on the other hand, is

▲ PLEASURE ISLAND DANCE CLUB

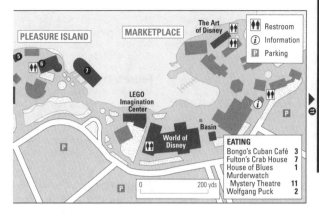

at least a twenty-minute drive away, and there's no public transport at night. The all-access ticket price encourages club-hopping, which is the best way to enjoy Pleasure Island. You can spend a short time at each club taking in the decor and atmosphere before deciding which one appeals most.

Marketplace

The rest of Downtown Disney consists of shops and restaurants in the appropriately named Marketplace, a bustling, open-air mall filled with browsing shoppers. Aside from the usual bunch of Disney stores, including the mother of all merchandise outlets, you can stock up on LEGO, gourmet chocolates, and smelly soaps, although bargains are difficult to find. The restaurants are mainly of the themed variety, and the menus are generally less adventurous than those at the West Side eateries.

Shops

Basin

Marketplace. Some of the most delicious (and expensive) bars

of soap that you'll ever smell are among the all-natural bath accessories and cosmetics sold here.

LEGO Imagination Center

Marketplace. Kids can play with all kinds of LEGO products while adults can admire the giant LEGO models of sea serpents, dinosaurs, and the like.

The Art of Disney

Marketplace. The watercolors, sculptures, and other limited-edition artwork of Disney characters and landmarks are

▲ LEGO IMAGINATION CENTER

several cuts above the usual merchandise, but you'd have to be a real connoisseur to fork out the many dollars (often in the hundreds) to own one.

Virgin Megastore

West Side. Music CDs of every style, DVDs, books, and numerous other multimedia products. Plenty of music listening posts provide a good way to kill some time.

World of Disney

Marketplace. More or less all of the cuddly toys, T-shirts, mugs, caps, and other overpriced souvenirs that you've seen for sale in the theme-park shops can be found here at the world's largest Disney merchandise store. Young girls will take great delight in visiting the Princess Room, full of items designed especially with them in mind.

Restaurants

Bongo's Cuban Café

West Side ☎ 407/828-0999. Owned by Latino pop stars Gloria and Emilio Estefan, the reasonable Cuban food is served up with

plenty of salsa, courtesy of live orchestras on Friday and Saturday evenings. Most main dishes are $15–20.

Fulton's Crab House

Marketplace ☎ 407/939-3463. Housed in a replica turn-of-the-century riverboat, this restaurant has some good, fresh seafood, although prices are steep, with lobster and crab dinners costing over $30.

House of Blues

West Side ☎ 407/934-2583, ☻ www .hob.com. In keeping with the jazz and blues played here (the restaurant has live music Thurs–Sat at 11pm), the food takes its inspiration from the Deep South, with decent attempts at dishes such as Cajun meatloaf and jambalaya, mostly in the $15–25 range. There is a popular Gospel Brunch every Sunday for $35.

Murderwatch Mystery Theatre

At the Grosvenor Hotel, next to Downtown Disney, 1850 Hotel Plaza Blvd ☎ 407/827-6534, ☻ www .murderwatch.com. Adults $39.95, children 9 & under $10.95. Shows on Sat only. The cast interacts with

▼ FULTON'S CRAB HOUSE

the audience in this Agatha Christie–style whodunit, which is played out in the dining room in between trips to the tasty prime-rib all-you-can-eat buffet.

Wolfgang Puck

West Side ☎407/938-9653. Four restaurants in one multilevel location: *The Dining Room* (dinner only); *The Café* for casual; *The Express* for self-service; and *B's Lounge & Sushi Bar* for sushi. At the lowest end of the price scale, you can tuck into pizza, rotisserie chicken, and savory sandwiches at *The Express* for around $10, while *The Dining Room* serves filet mignon, veal cutlets and such, prepared in a gourmet style for $20–35.

Bars and clubs

8TRAX

Pleasure Island. Revolving disco balls are much in evidence at this dance club where 1970s music is the order of all nights except Thursdays, when an equally kitsch selection of 1980s tracks are given airing.

Adventurers Club

Pleasure Island. This is the most original – and enjoyable – nightspot on Pleasure Island, loosely based on a 1930s gentlemen's club and furnished with a motley collection of wall masks (some of which unexpectedly start speaking), deer heads, and assorted flea-market furniture. Between scheduled shows that take place every twenty minutes or so throughout the evening – including everything from cabarets to Balderdash competitions – actors and actresses move surreptitiously (despite their period attire) among the crowd and strike up loud and eccentric conversations with unsuspecting audience members.

BET Soundstage Club

Pleasure Island. Thurs–Sat must be 21 or over to enter, Sun–Wed must be 18 or over. Owned by Black Entertainment Television and possibly Pleasure Island's most popular club on account of the hip-hop and R&B it plays.

Comedy Warehouse

Pleasure Island. Four shows nightly Sun–Wed, five shows nightly Thurs–Sat. The comedians have to keep the jokes clean and suitable for all ages, but are not afraid to send up Mickey and friends every now and then. Plenty of improvisation and audience interaction. Each show lasts about thirty minutes.

House of Blues

West Side ☎407/934-2583, ⊛www .hob.com. Shows usually start between 7–9pm. Backed financially by the Blues Brothers themselves, plus other celebrities such as Aerosmith, the 2000-seat Music Hall concert venue showcases the talents of top soul, blues, and rock 'n' roll artists from around the world.

Mannequins Dance Palace

Pleasure Island. Thurs–Sat must be 21 or over to enter, Sun–Wed must be 18 or over. Notable for its massive rotating dance floor and the best lighting and sound systems of any of the Pleasure Island clubs, this is Disney at its most risqué. Electronic dance music dominates and the place rarely gets going until around midnight.

▲ CIRQUE DU SOLEIL

Motion

Pleasure Island. It seems as though the ideas were running thin when this club was devised, resulting in a tepid stream of top-40 tunes and a large screen showing music videos.

Rock 'n' Roll Beach Club

Pleasure Island. The only club to offer occasional live bands along with the DJs. Golden oldies are the staple here, played in a club based on a beach-party theme.

Live shows

Cirque du Soleil

West Side ☎ 407/939-1298, ⊛ www
.cirquedusoleil.com. Shows Tues–Sat
6pm & 9pm. Adults $59–87, children
3–9 $44–65. The Cirque du
Soleil has made Downtown Disney its permanent home, presenting its fascinating 90-minute show *La Nouba* in a 1600-seat theater ten times a week. A tapestry of life and its emotions rather than a conventional story with a beginning, middle, and end, the show takes you on a journey through an offbeat world where dreams and reality intertwine. The show features the company's famed acrobats and gymnasts performing feats of strength, agility, and coordination, against a backdrop of surreal sets. The elaborate costumes, music, and choreography add greatly to the experience. The one drawback: as good as the show is, the prices seem a little high for what you get.

Universal Studios

Like Disney, Universal's theme-park presence in Florida results from a similar successful venture in California. In Universal's case, it was a tour of its studios in Los Angeles, which they reprised in Orlando in 1990. Subsequent multi-million-dollar cash infusions have turned Universal Studios into a full-fledged theme park – which also functions as a working production studio – similar in style and scale to Disney-MGM Studios. The rides, most of which are based on disaster films, horror movies, or action flicks, appeal especially to an adult audience. Little attempt has been made to water down their intensity (as Disney has a tendency to do), and the special effects are superb.

The park itself is arranged around a large lagoon and nominally divided into several areas. New York, Hollywood, San Francisco, and Amity (the New England town where Jaws took place) are impeccably replicated in street sets; New York is especially authentic. Production Central, World Expo, and Woody Woodpecker's KidZone are less distinctive, containing lots of attractions but little eye-catching scenery.

Shrek 4-D

Production Central. Conceived before the movie *Shrek 2* came out, this delightful 3-D presentation continues where the original movie finished. If you missed *Shrek*, watch carefully as the basic plot is explained on a Magic Mirror (à la *Snow White*) in the lobby before you enter the theater. However, even if you are unfamiliar with – or don't care about – the storyline, the wonderful animated graphics, accompanied by more "feelies" than any other 3-D attraction in Orlando (including a few too many water sprays), are totally enthralling.

Jimmy Neutron's Nicktoon Blast

Production Central. Minimum height 40"/102cm. This hugely popular attraction, helped perhaps by its location near the park entrance, uses flight-simulator technology to good effect, but less impressively than the park's *Back to the Future The Ride*,

For park hours and prices, see "Theme park practicalities" in Essentials.

▲ AUDIENCE WATCHING SHREK 4-D

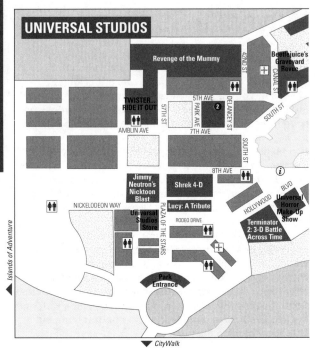

UNIVERSAL STUDIOS

Islands of Adventure ◀

Universal Studios PLACES

Revenge of the Mummy

42ND ST

Beetlejuice's Graveyard Revue

CANAL ST

TWISTER... RIDE IT OUT

5TH AVE

PARK AVE

57TH ST

DELANCEY ST

2

SOUTH ST

AMBLIN AVE

7TH AVE

SOUTH ST

8TH AVE

ⓘ

BLVD

Jimmy Neutron's Nicktoon Blast

Shrek 4-D

NICKELODEON WAY

Lucy: A Tribute

HOLLYWOOD

Universal Horror Make-Up Show

Universal Studios Store

PLAZA OF THE STARS

RODEO DRIVE

Terminator 2: 3-D Battle Across Time

Park Entrance

▼ *CityWalk*

which uses similar technology. The best part of the ride is the animated graphics that take you on a journey featuring a panoply of other Nickelodeon cartoon characters such as SpongeBob and The Rugrats. The screen, however, is set too far back from your "Rocket Pod," so that often you feel like you're simply watching Jimmy's

adventures in a cinema rather than actually doing them with him.

Revenge of the Mummy

New York. Minimum height 48"/122cm. The park's newest ride – and only rollercoaster – starts off slowly as you travel through scenes from the eponymous movie, and never

Saving time

Two major attractions, **Shrek 4-D** and **Jimmy Neutron's Nicktoon Blast**, lie just beyond the park entrance. Since Universal Express passes (see p.173) for these two run out quickly on busy days, get the pass for one of these attractions (Shrek 4-D is more worthwhile) before going further into the park. Don't bother getting a Universal Express pass for shows or attractions that run to fixed times (such as Terminator 2: 3-D Battle Across Time); just turn up ten minutes or so before the scheduled show time. There are single-rider lines, reserved for people boarding solo – which involve little or no waiting time – for Revenge of the Mummy and MEN IN BLACK Alien Attack.

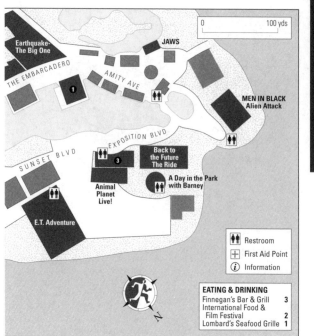

Key on map:

JAWS

Earthquake-The Big One

THE EMBARCADERO

AMITY AVE

MEN IN BLACK Alien Attack

EXPOSITION BLVD

SUNSET BLVD

Back to the Future The Ride

A Day in the Park with Barney

Animal Planet Live!

E.T. Adventure

0 100 yds

👫 Restroom
➕ First Aid Point
ⓘ Information

EATING & DRINKING
Finnegan's Bar & Grill 3
International Food &
 Film Festival 2
Lombard's Seafood Grille 1

speeds up enough to satiate hardcore thrillseekers. There are some memorable moments, however, such as when your coaster is attacked by fireballs and then takes an unexpected backward plunge into darkness. You can avoid the usually very long lines by entering as a single rider.

TWISTER...RIDE IT OUT

New York. The awesome power of a tornado is re-created superbly in a few devastating minutes in this short attraction padded with some preliminary footage of how the movie *Twister* was made. After the film, you walk on to a movie set and witness (in a sheltered spot) the wind, rain, and eventually the tornado itself tear through a small Oklahoma town. The effects are frighteningly realistic, except, that is, for the cow hanging from a rope that flies past you in the midst of the storm.

Earthquake – The Big One

San Francisco/Amity. This attraction, vaguely akin to Disney-MGM Studios' Backlot Tour, starts off with a methodical and not particularly riveting explanation of how movie special effects have evolved over the years, focusing on the 1974 film *Earthquake* starring Charlton Heston, in which buildings were made to rock simply by shaking the cameras. You then board a San Francisco subway train and enter a scene from the movie, where much more sophisticated special effects give

▲ REVENGE OF THE MUMMY

you a terrifying idea of what it would feel like to be caught underground when an 8.3 Richter-scale quake hits.

JAWS

San Francisco/Amity. The nerve-jangling *Jaws* theme makes this one of the park's more popular attractions. There are some good special effects, notably the exploding petrol station towards the end of the ride, as an abnormally large and nasty shark disrupts your boat-tour through Amity's normally peaceful waters. Although the shark keeps you on edge by looming unexpectedly out of the water, there are few really scary moments, and the whole thing ends rather abruptly without giving you the time to be fully absorbed in the adventure.

MEN IN BLACK Alien Attack

World Expo. Minimum height 42"/107cm. The one good thing about this ride is that there is a single-rider line. Otherwise, it's really not worth waiting long in the normal line for what turns out to be a rather

inane experience. The idea is to zap as many aliens as you can, accumulating points after each successful shot in an attempt to pass your MIB agent training. Since you don't get a coherent explication of the game's rules, you never really know when and what you have hit. Therefore, you'll enjoy the ride just as much if you simply sit back and watch the well-designed monsters try to frighten you.

Back to the Future The Ride

World Expo. Minimum height 40"/102cm. Notwithstanding the recent addition of Revenge of the Mummy, this remains the park's most exciting attraction. The excellent visual effects are the main reason why this flight-simulator ride succeeds when other lesser rides using the same technology are little more than a series of jerks and bumps. Without resorting to 3-D imagery, your time machine flies across primeval landscapes, through the Ice Age, and back to the future with tremendous realism as you chase the mischievous Biff, who has stolen one of Dr. Brown's machines.

E.T. Adventure

Woody Woodpecker's KidZone. Your mission is to take E.T. home so that he can save his dying planet. Aside from bicycle buggies that give the impression that you are flying, there is not much to commend the ride – this one will appeal mostly to small children, much like the other rides in Woody Woodpecker's KidZone. The waiting line winds through a forest full of E.T.-like characters, including Botanicus, a wise elder from E.T.'s planet, providing a welcome distraction as you wait your turn. And E.T. saying your name at the end of the adventure is a nice touch that anyone might appreciate.

Terminator 2: 3-D Battle Across Time

Hollywood. After a lengthy presentation of the megalomaniac corporation Cyberdyne Systems' vision of the future, complete with battery-operated butterflies, a Ronald Reagan–style missile defense system, and robot soldiers, you are led into a theater to witness the ensuing battle between the machines and two hapless humans aided by Arnold Schwarzenegger's Terminator character. Even though the show is relatively long and uses a good mixture of live action, special effects, and 3-D imagery, the overall effect is only marginally more interesting than watching the movie in the cinema.

Other rides and attractions

The rest of the park merits only a cursory glance. This might prove tricky for those with kids in tow, since youngsters will gravitate naturally to the playgrounds and fairground rides of Woody Woodpecker's KidZone and will want to stay there far too long for most parents' liking. A good carrot to get them off the rides is **A Day in the Park with Barney**, a show where the youngest of visitors will enjoy singing and clapping along with Barney and company in an enchanting "forest" in-the-round. At the other end of the age scale, grown-ups old enough to remember Lucille Ball will enjoy **Lucy: A Tribute**, a museum-style exhibit (with no wait) featuring clips, props, costumes, and the like.

Shops

Universal Studios Store

Plaza of the Stars, Production Central. Your one-stop-shop for Universal merchandise, where you'll find a bit of everything, from Spider-Man to SpongeBob. Since this store stocks most of what you'll find elsewhere in the park and is conveniently close to the

▼ JAWS

entrance, consider making your purchases here just before leaving the park.

Restaurants

Finnegan's Bar & Grill
5th Ave, New York. This place has a convivial atmosphere for a theme park restaurant, thanks mainly to its live Irish music and 4–7pm happy hour. Guinness is served on tap, while pale imitations of fish and chips, shepherd's pie, and other Anglo-Saxon specialties are served in two dining rooms for $10–13. The dining room with its entrance on 5th Avenue is cozier than the one on Delancey Street.

International Food and Film Festival
Exposition Blvd, World Expo. Despite the promising name, this self-service restaurant offers just a few mediocre Oriental stir-fries ($8.50) and wonton soup ($3.50) in addition to its burgers and pizzas, making it only marginally more cosmopolitan than the park's other eateries. The decor is sterile, but you can eat your food while watching movies, including classics and foreign films.

Lombard's Seafood Grille
The Embarcadero, San Francisco/Amity. The park's smartest restaurant is for seafood lovers, where $15–20 buys you a decent lobster risotto, shrimp alfredo, or a basket of clams. You can either eat inside or alfresco on a terrace overlooking the lagoon, peacefully away from the general hubbub.

▲ UNIVERSAL HORROR MAKE-UP SHOW

Live shows

Animal Planet Live!
Woody Woodpecker's KidZone. Lacking the charm and diversity of animals at SeaWorld Orlando's excellent *Pets Ahoy!*, this twenty-minute show basically has dogs doing a handful of undemanding tricks, with cameo appearances by a chimpanzee and an orangutan.

Beetlejuice's Graveyard Revue
San Francisco/Amity. High-tempo renditions of *I Will Survive*, *It's Raining Men*, *YMCA*, and other catchy tunes are performed by a cast of monsters. Although lacking in imagination, the show is watchable, as much for the risqué humor as for the song and dance.

Universal Horror Make-Up Show
Hollywood. All-round the park's best show reveals some of the secrets of horror-movie special effects, a subject matter which lends itself especially well to tasteless (but often funny) jokes that tend to be raunchier than the usual theme-park humor, as well as revealing the squeamish nature of young (often female) volunteers from the crowd.

Islands of Adventure

Just a five-minute walk from Universal Studios lies Islands of Adventure, which continues Universal's emphasis on fast, occasionally rollicking, rides for adults. The preponderance of excellent thrill rides sets Islands of Adventure apart from all other Orlando theme parks and outshines anything that Disney has to offer in this department. The park is divided into five sections, each with their own unique character: Marvel Super Hero Island and The Lost Continent have the most exciting rides, molded on the comic-book heroes of your youth and ancient myths and legends respectively. Jurassic Park goes to town on the well-worn dinosaur motif in a scientific as well as scary way; Toon Lagoon uses cartoon characters to get you completely soaked; and the eye-catching Seuss Landing is where the kids can spin about on a variety of fairground-style rides.

Incredible Hulk Coaster

Marvel Super Hero Island. Minimum height 54"/137cm. While definitely a rollercoaster to be reckoned with, the loop-the-loops and plunges on this one would be far scarier if they were higher up. As it is, the ride satisfies without seriously making you want to regurgitate your lunch. By far the best part is the start: a high-speed catapult launch that apparently has the same thrust as an F-16 fighter jet. Two unexpected tunnels also give the ride some welcome variety.

Doctor Doom's Fearfall

Marvel Super Hero Island. Minimum height 52"/132cm. This ride lasts

For park hours and prices, see "Theme park practicalities" in Essentials.

barely a minute, with the first few seconds the only thrilling part as you are shot 150 feet into the air and experience a moment of weightlessness on the way down. After this brief adrenaline rush, there is little more to do than enjoy the panoramic views over the park. The single-rider line, which can usually get you onto the ride with no wait, is accessed through the video arcade next to the ride's main entrance.

Saving time

Upon entering the park, turn left and grab a Universal Express pass for the **Incredible Hulk Coaster**. Then consider touring the park in an anti-clockwise direction, against the general flow of traffic. This will also get you to the park's other popular rollercoaster, **Dueling Dragons**, quicker than if you were to go clockwise. The two other thrill rides, **The Amazing Adventures of Spider-Man** and **Doctor Doom's Fearfall**, are near the entrance, but since they both have single-rider lines – which involve little or no waiting time – they can be left til later.

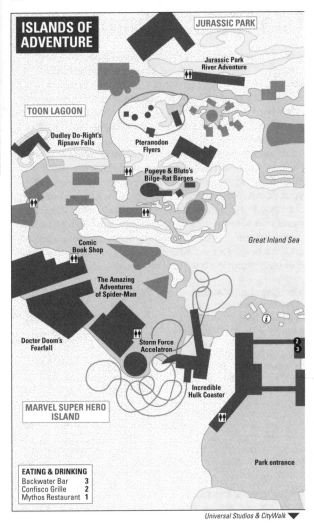

ISLANDS OF ADVENTURE

JURASSIC PARK

Jurassic Park
River Adventure

TOON LAGOON

Dudley Do-Right's
Ripsaw Falls

Pteranodon
Flyers

Popeye & Bluto's
Bilge-Rat Barges

Great Inland Sea

Comic
Book Shop

The Amazing
Adventures
of Spider-Man

Doctor Doom's
Fearfall

Storm Force
Accelatron

Incredible
Hulk Coaster

MARVEL SUPER HERO
ISLAND

Park entrance

EATING & DRINKING	
Backwater Bar	3
Confisco Grille	2
Mythos Restaurant	1

Universal Studios & CityWalk ▼

The Amazing Adventures of Spider-Man

Marvel Super Hero Island. Minimum height 40"/102cm. This is one of the best rides in Orlando. The ever-popular Spider-Man theme is a major draw in itself, but it is the way in which the super hero's escapades are brought so vividly to life that makes this ride stand out. Your buggy moves at a fast pace (though not rollercoaster-fast) through a high-rise city where Spider-Man battles against a variety of villains. With the aid of superb 3-D imagery (don't forget to pick up your glasses

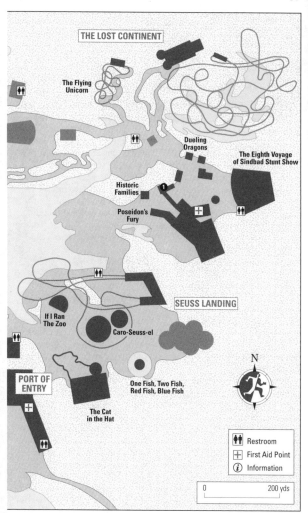

THE LOST CONTINENT

The Flying
Unicorn

Dueling
Dragons

The Eighth Voyage
of Sindbad Stunt Show

Historic
Families

Poseidon's
Fury

SEUSS LANDING

If I Ran
The Zoo

Caro-Seuss-el

N

PORT OF
ENTRY

One Fish, Two Fish,
Red Fish, Blue Fish

The Cat
in the Hat

Restroom
First Aid Point
Information

0   200 yds

just before boarding the buggy)
and the occasional sensory
effect such as a blast of hot
air or spurt of water, you are
drawn completely into the story.
Another great thing about this
ride is that you can get on it
very quickly by using the single-
rider line.

Dudley Do-Right's Ripsaw Falls

Toon Lagoon. Minimum height
44"/112cm. Thanks to the
the final 60-foot drop in a
hollowed-out-log boat that
thoroughly drenches all four
passengers, this attraction has
the dubious reputation of being

PLACES

Islands of Adventure

▲ INCREDIBLE HULK COASTER

one of Orlando's wettest rides away from the water parks. Before the final drop, you're peppered with sprays and splashes of water as you ride along various waterways in Dudley's hometown of Ripsaw Falls, which looks interesting from the outside, but contains disappointingly little to look at during the ride itself. You really will get soaked from head to toe on this one, so consider bypassing it on cooler days when it takes longer to dry off.

Jurassic Park River Adventure

Jurassic Park. Minimum height 42"/107cm. Based on the Jurassic Park films, this ride substitutes a boat for a 4WD vehicle as you take a tour through a primeval zoo. The first part of the trip is your standard jaunt past several quite realistic dinosaurs lolling their heads up and down and baring teeth – not overly exciting. Things liven up when the raptor containment area is breached and various carnivorous beasts are on the loose, providing the cue for some decent special effects, pyrotechnics, and ultimately an unexpected 85-foot drop.

Dueling Dragons

The Lost Continent. Minimum height 54"/137cm. This is actually two rollercoasters, "Fire" and

"Ice" (separate waiting lines for each; turn left for "Fire" and right for "Ice"), starting off parallel to one another, but then diverging to follow their own paths. Each ride is of a similar intensity and involves harrowing near-misses with the other coaster, which makes sitting in the front row especially thrilling (there is a special – and longer – waiting line for front-row riders). If all of this wasn't enough, the seats leave your feet dangling precariously in mid-air, adding to the sense of danger.

Poseidon's Fury

The Lost Continent. Trapped in Poseidon's temple, you and your wisecracking guide have to survive the wrath of the gods in order to escape. This involves passing through several chambers on foot, edging closer and closer to Poseidon and his nemesis, Lord Darkenon, who are both itching to have a fight. The final battle scene is played out on a huge wrap-around screen, with plenty of real-life fireballs exploding in front of you, but the highlight comes earlier on in the adventure when, in order to get from one chamber to another, you have to pass through a vortex of raging water. This attraction works well provided you have the patience to follow the plot; if your mind wanders, however, it can quickly become a little pointless.

Seuss Landing

This area of the park re-creates the wacky world of Dr Seuss, and as such the rides are designed for children. Take a few minutes, however, to stroll

▲ POSEIDON'S FURY

an enchanted forest. In Toon Lagoon, **Popeye & Bluto's Bilge-Rat Barges** is a raft ride where, potentially at least, you stay dryer than Dudley Do-Right's Ripsaw Falls (see p.97); the major threat comes from malevolent spectators who pay 25 cents to release jets of water on passing rafts. The Jurassic Park area has an unexciting Dinosaur Discovery center with several interactive exhibits, as well as a multi-level playground full of bones and fossils. The hang-glider-style gondolas that fly over the playground are **The Pteranodon Flyers**, a fun-looking diversion which, unfortunately for grown-ups, can only be enjoyed if you are accompanied by a child between 36 and 56 inches tall.

past the incredibly colorful scenery, admiring the way in which the architects have managed to avoid building anything in a straight line. **The Cat in the Hat** retells the famous story as you ride past various show scenes in spinning sofas, while the other attractions continue the Seussian theme: **Caro-Seuss-el** is a standard merry-go-round; **If I Ran the Zoo** an interactive playground; and **One Fish, Two Fish, Red Fish, Blue Fish** a Flying Dumbo–style ride where the twist is that you can control the height of your flight so as to avoid being hit by water that squirts in time to the accompanying song.

Shops

Comic Book Shop

Marvel Super Hero Island. A great place for comic lovers, with

▼ SEUSS LANDING

Other rides and attractions

Elsewhere in the park there are a couple of mild thrill rides for all ages: in Marvel Super Hero Island, **Storm Force Accelatron** involves cars spinning and whirling to a noisy light show; and The Lost Continent's **The Flying Unicorn** is a mini-rollercoaster which takes you on a fanciful flight through

books and magazines recounting the adventures of super-hero celebrities such as Spider-Man and The Incredible Hulk, as well as lesser-known B-Listers including She-Hulk, Iron Man, and Black Panther.

Historic Families

The Lost Continent. The heraldic charts and family-name histories probably sell better, but the swords and daggers – sometimes costing several hundred dollars – make for more enjoyable window shopping. There are also some classy chess sets for sale.

Restaurants

Confisco Grille

Port of Entry. The dark, themed dining room evokes some far-flung Customs House with various exotic confiscated items on display. Unfortunately the food is rather more mundane, with ordinary fajitas ($14.99–17.99) and bland Pad Thai ($14.99) the most daring dishes on the menu.

▲ COMIC BOOK SHOP

▲ MYTHOS RESTAURANT

Mythos Restaurant

The Lost Continent. Consistently rated as one of Orlando's best theme-park restaurants, the interior decor, resembling the inside of an extinct volcano, feels a bit tacky for the varied, upscale cuisine on offer. The menu changes regularly, but usually includes a couple of filling pasta dishes, a good *coq au vin*, and thin-crusted wood-fired pizzas. All main courses are under $20.

Bars

Backwater Bar

Port of Entry. Adjoining the *Confisco Grille*, this snug, rather nondescript bar with a few outdoor tables has a selection of alcoholic drinks that is, bizarrely, limited to one per adult guest.

Live shows

The Eighth Voyage of Sindbad Stunt Show

The Lost Continent. The park's one live show is an ambitious one in which Sindbad endeavors to rescue a princess from an evil witch. This quest is played out on an elaborate set using plenty of stunts, but it is the pyrotechnics that are most impressive.

CityWalk

CityWalk is Universal's attempt to make its mark on the Orlando nightlife scene. Without the hyper-wholesome image that Disney has to live up to, it manages to be a hipper alternative to Downtown Disney – and also a less expensive one. On the whole, though, it's all rather tame, and the bars, nightclubs, and themed restaurants that are spread over two open-air levels on a wedge of land between Universal Studios and Islands of Adventure have all been done very much with the tourist in mind. Indeed, compared to downtown Orlando's extensive and eclectic after-dark options, CityWalk can seem a little sterile and monotonous. Still, it's convenient if you're staying on Universal property or along nearby International Drive, and you'll find more than enough bustling nightspots to keep you entertained.

Hard Rock Café

6050 Universal Blvd ☎407/351-ROCK. While there are certainly better places to eat in CityWalk than here, this *Hard Rock Café* does hold the distinction of being the world's largest. The overpriced burgers and sandwiches are served in a two-floored, 600-seat dining area with wall-to-wall rock 'n' roll memorabilia and a revolving pink Cadillac smack in the middle – all very typical of the *Hard Rock* genre. The restaurant, as well as the adjoining 3000-capacity Hard Rock Live concert venue (see p.106), are housed in

a realistic interpretation of Rome's Coliseum, adding some welcome architectural interest to CityWalk's generally quite

▼ CITYWALK HORSE CARRIAGES

CityWalk practicalities

CityWalk (☎407/363-8000, ⊛www.citywalkorlando.com) is open daily 11–2am. The **CityWalk Party Pass** costs only $9.95 ($13 if you want to take in a movie) and includes all-night access to *Jimmy Buffett's Margaritaville, Bob Marley – A Tribute to Freedom, Latin Quarter, Pat O'Brien's, CityJazz,* and *the groove*. Otherwise, individual cover charges to the clubs are $5–8. You must be at least 18 to enter the clubs, and 21 at *Bob Marley – A Tribute to Freedom* (after 10pm), *Pat O'Brien's* (after 9pm), and *the groove* (all night). Parking costs $9 during the day, but is free after 6pm.

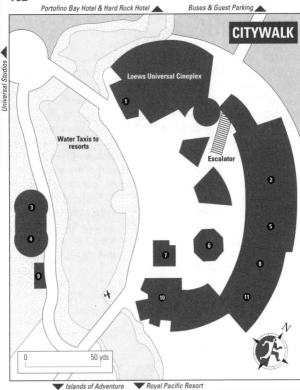

Portofino Bay Hotel & Hard Rock Hotel ▲   Buses & Guest Parking ▲

CITYWALK

◄ Universal Studios

PLACES

CityWalk

Loews Universal Cineplex

1

Escalator

Water Taxis to resorts

2

3

5

4

6

9

7

8

10

11

N

| 0 | 50 yds |

▼ Islands of Adventure   ▼ Royal Pacific Resort

CLUBS & LIVE MUSIC		EATING & DRINKING	
Bob Marley – A Tribute to Freedom	2	Bob Marley – A Tribute to Freedom	2
CityJazz	6	Emeril's	7
Hard Rock Live	4	Hard Rock Café	3
Jimmy Buffett's Margaritaville	10	Jimmy Buffett's Margaritaville	10
Latin Quarter	11	Latin Quarter	11
Pat O'Brien's	5	NASCAR Café	1
the groove	8	NBA City	9
		Pat O'Brien's	5

▲ HARD ROCK CAFÉ

unremarkable collection of buildings.

Loews Universal Cineplex

6000 Universal Blvd ☎407/354-3374. Tickets $6–8.25. With the majority of Orlando's cinema complexes scattered around the city in inconveniently located shopping malls, this ultra-modern, twenty-screen complex with reasonable ticket prices and the usual

▲ WATER TAXIS

selection of Hollywood films is something to consider after an energy-sapping day at one of the Universal theme parks. You can combine a movie with either access to all of CityWalk's clubs for $13 or a meal at one of the following six restaurants for $19.95: *Jimmy Buffet's Margaritaville*, *Hard Rock Café*, *Latin Quarter*, *NASCAR Café*, *NBA City* (for these restaurants, see p.104), or *Pastamoré*, a rather ordinary Italian restaurant.

Water taxis

The best thing about the water taxis that dock at a jetty in the center of CityWalk is that they're free. The taxis ply the waters to and from the three resorts on Universal property (see p.162), and the people who use them are assumed to be guests of the hotels; however, there is no check. The trip itself is a pleasant, gentle one along quiet waterways, giving a general overview of Universal property and providing a pleasant way of escaping the crowds for half an hour or so. One of the highlights comes when you pull into the "bay" of the sleepy Italian seaside village that is the *Portofino Bay Hotel*.

Shops

Cigarz at CityWalk

CityWalk, 6000 Universal Blvd. Novelty smokes as well as quality cigars are on sale at this store decorated to resemble an old Cuban cigar factory. Smoking is permitted in the small bar at the back, which sells a reasonable range of alcholic drinks and is a quiet, out-of-the-way alternative to the busier nightspots.

The Endangered Species Store

6000 Universal Blvd. A merchandise store where the T-shirts are made from recycled cotton and the cuddly toys and statues – some of them quite tasteful and attractive – are of animals threatened by extinction.

▲ BOB MARLEY - A TRIBUTE TO FREEDOM

Restaurants

Bob Marley – A Tribute to Freedom

6000 Universal Blvd ☏407/224-3663.
Featuring a fairly representative cross-section of Jamaican cuisine, much of it prepared with spicy jerk seasoning and served in relatively small portions. The fish dishes – snapper, tuna, corvina, and the like – are generally more substantial and cost around $15. Once the live musical entertainment starts at around 8pm, the emphasis shifts from eating to drinking and dancing.

Emeril's

6000 Universal Blvd
☏407/224-2424, ⊛www
.emerils.com.
CityWalk's most upscale restaurant is overseen by TV chef Emeril Lagasse. The dining room is simple – even a little austere – but the food, featuring a lot of New Orleans creations such as cráb cakes and smoked duck with a Bourbon-caramel glaze, is top-notch. Most dinner entrees cost $28–34. Reservations are required.

Jimmy Buffett's Margaritaville

6000 Universal Blvd ☏407/224-2155, ⊛www.margaritaville.com /orlando. Reasonably priced Caribbean-style food such as jerk salmon and coconut shrimp (both $14.95) served in an appropriately tropical setting, complete with a volcano exploding with margarita mix, which sets the scene for the energetic atmosphere that prevails here.

▲ EMERIL'S

Latin Quarter

6000 Universal Blvd ☎407/224-3663. Traditional dishes of Latin America – defined broadly to include nachos, fajitas, and barbecue ribs – are given a "Nuevo Latino" contemporary touch, including a sumptuous paella containing several different types of seafood and chorizo. Most main dishes cost $15–20.

NASCAR Café

6000 Universal Blvd ☎407/224-7223, ⊛www.nascarcafeorlando .com. There is nothing extraordinary about the burgers and sandwiches (around $10) or the ribs and steaks ($15–20) served in this two-floor restaurant cluttered with NASCAR memorabilia, including cars suspended from the ceiling and TV footage of famous moments in this hugely popular sport.

NBA City

6860 Universal Blvd ☎407/363-5919, ⊛www.nbacity.com. Boasting more imaginative cuisine than is found at most themed restaurants, including chicken blue-cheese pasta ($13.95) and herb-roasted pork loin ($10.95), *NBA City* also features an interactive area where you can test your basketball-throwing skills and see how high you can jump.

Pat O'Brien's

6000 Universal Blvd ☎407/224-2106, ⊛www.patobriens.com/orlando .html. Re-creating perfectly the feel of Old New Orleans, with wrought-iron balconies and a relaxing outdoor patio with plenty of shade – the best place to enjoy decent, moderately priced dishes such as jambalaya ($11.95) and crawfish nachos ($12.95).

▲ NBA CITY

Clubs and live music

Bob Marley – A Tribute to Freedom

6000 Universal Blvd ☎407/224-3663. The house band plays passable covers of Marley songs, as well as other reggae tunes, and the place is usually very busy at weekends. Cocktails are predictably heavy on the rum, and you can also enjoy Jamaica's Red Stripe beer.

▼ PAT O'BRIEN'S

▲ THE GROOVE

CityJazz

6000 Universal Blvd ☎407/224-2189. Ironically, there is little jazz to be heard at this intimate nightclub, decorated attractively in soft colors with tables around a stage. The live bands tend to play mainstream rock music, although there is plenty of jazz memorabilia plastered on the walls.

the groove

6000 Universal Blvd. Cover charge $5. CityWalk's only full-fledged dance club has a good sound system, plenty of flashing lights, and a huge dance floor where you can hear various styles of music which become more electronic as the night progresses. Three differently colored rooms (decorated in red, green, and blue) provide quieter spots for the generally young crowd to chill out; and the occasional alcohol-free "teen night" from around 8pm to midnight gives adolescents their chance on the floor.

Hard Rock Live

6050 Universal Blvd ☎407/351-LIVE, ⊛www.hardrocklive.com. Box office daily 10am–9pm. Ticket prices vary: usually $35–65 for a big-name artist. One of Orlando's major concert venues, this 3000-capacity auditorium – less grandiose inside than its Roman Coliseum exterior would suggest, but with a large stage and special effects galore – showcases musical acts (mainly rock bands), some of them famous, others hoping to be.

Jimmy Buffett's Margaritaville

6000 Universal Blvd ☎407/224-2155, ⊛www .margaritaville.com/orlando. High-tempo, infectious island-style music performed live nightly, plus the possibility of downing several different types of potent margarita from $6 and up, make staying on after dinner a tempting proposition at this lively bar-restaurant.

Latin Quarter

6000 Universal Blvd ☎407/224-3663. Salseros and lovers of other Latin dances can practice their moves to the accompaniment of live orchestras and DJs Thursday–Saturday at this happening spot that doubles as a Latino restaurant. Impromptu classes are sometimes offered for beginners, but more advanced dancers may find it difficult to find partners of the appropriate level among the crowd.

Pat O'Brien's

6000 Universal Blvd ☎407/224-2106, ⊛www.patobriens.com/orlando.html. This restaurant's piano bar is the focal point of the evening, as two musicians sit at baby grand pianos facing each other on a small stage playing songs requested by the audience – which tends to be older than at other CityWalk bars – each one trying to outdo the other. A good sing-along usually ensues.

SeaWorld Orlando and Discovery Cove

SeaWorld Orlando is the pick of Florida's numerous marine parks and should not be missed. While it lacks the magical atmosphere of Disney and the exciting rides of Universal, it makes up for these deficiencies by presenting its huge collection of animals simply and stylishly in aquariums, pools, tanks, and carefully re-created natural habitats dotted around the park. The highlights are the large stadiums that play host to superb live shows featuring sea lions and killer whales. SeaWorld also has the towering steel Kraken, one of the best rollercoasters in Orlando. Much more wildlife can be found across the road at Discovery Cove, owned, like SeaWorld, by Anheuser-Busch and a little different from anything else in Orlando. A theme park without a theme, a water park without the slides, an aquarium without the glass tank, here the emphasis is on getting up close and personal with the animals. Swimming with dolphins is the star attraction, while pools filled with tropical fish and rays plus a colorful aviary provide further opportunities for nature encounters.

Stingray Lagoon

SeaWorld. Situated near SeaWorld's entrance, this is the first of several smaller displays that play a supporting role to the large-scale shows and rides, but are well worth a look in their own right. The appeal here is that you can enjoy a fair amount of interaction with the animals. The amazingly sociable rays in this shallow pool have had their stingers removed, but are kept happy by visitors ready to fork out $4 to feed them plates of fish.

Dolphin Cove and Dolphin Nursery

SeaWorld. The interactive Dolphin Cove demonstrates the comfort level of dolphins in the company of humans (especially humans with fistfuls of fish). These playful creatures let themselves be stroked while gliding along the sides of a large pool on the prowl for their next snack. The nearby Dolphin Nursery is a more tranquil setting where barriers around the pool prevent people from petting the calves kept here – the fruit of SeaWorld's dolphin-breeding program.

Manatees: The Last Generation?

SeaWorld. Don't miss the chance

For park hours and prices, see "Theme park practicalities" in Essentials.

SeaWorld Orlando and Discovery Cove

to get a close-quarters look at these imposing, lettuce-munching mammals, which can sometimes grow to thirteen feet and a whopping 3500 pounds. Manatees are endangered in Florida's waters primarily by accidents with boats and man-made pollution. The initial viewing is from an outside walkway, but you can get better, underwater views by entering the complex itself, where you can also watch a short film about the manatee's modern-day plight. All of the

Saving time

SeaWorld Orlando lacks any FASTPASS-style scheme; then again, it also lacks the kind of attractions that involve long waiting lines. **Kraken**, **Journey to Atlantis**, and the flight-simulator ride at **Wild Arctic** are the only times when you will have to wait to experience an attraction. The best tactic, then, is to go on these rides during one of the hugely popular live-animal shows, when the number of people milling about the park can be significantly reduced.

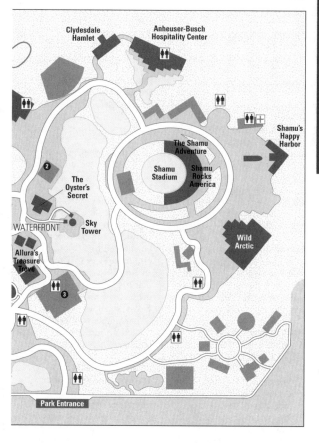

Clydesdale Hamlet

Anheuser-Busch Hospitality Center

Shamu's Happy Harbor

The Shamu Adventure

Shamu Stadium

Shamu Rocks America

2

The Oyster's Secret

WATERFRONT

Sky Tower

Allura's Treasure Trove

3

Wild Arctic

Park Entrance

manatees here were rescued by SeaWorld's animal rescue team, and this attraction doubles as the world's largest manatee rehabilitation facility.

Journey to Atlantis SeaWorld.
Minimum height: 42"/107cm.
The park's first thrill ride is billed as a "water coaster" by virtue of the fact that you travel on both water and rails, but it never really lives up to the hype. The "coaster" part of the ride is neither fast nor exciting, and the only notable moment is one sheer drop that will soak

▼ JOURNEY TO ATLANTIS

everyone in the front row. Upon exiting the ride, take a few minutes to look at the two aquariums in the adjacent gift shop: one underfoot with stingrays, the other overhead with hammerhead sharks.

Kraken

SeaWorld. Minimum height: 52"/132cm. Traveling at breakneck speeds of up to 65mph on seven loop-the-loops that go as high as a fifteen-story building, this ride is a candidate for Orlando's best rollercoaster. Enjoy the bird's-eye views as the coaster climbs to its starting point high above the park, since for the rest of the time your eyes will be shut tight. The fact that your legs are left dangling in midair throughout the entire ride raises the fear factor another few notches.

Pacific Point Preserve

SeaWorld. While the stingrays and dolphins will happily devour any fish thrown their way, it is the California sea lions and harbor seals kept in this large tank complete with the rocks and grottoes of their native Pacific coastline that do the most to earn their dinner, posing on rocks until you decide to toss them a morsel, which they catch in their mouths with great dexterity. Underwater viewing also allows you to witness their speed and agility closer up.

Penguin Encounter

SeaWorld. Penguins are surprisingly graceful underwater, darting around like bulbous black arrows, while on land they exhibit the peculiar mannerisms they're so well known for – the waddling, slipping on the ice, and knocking each other over. All this combines to make them real crowd-pleasers. Four different species – king, gentoo, chinstrap, and rockhopper – can be enjoyed here (along with puffins) as they cavort around an Antarctic environment that has been re-created with great attention to detail – right down to being more dimly lit in summer to mimic light conditions in the South Pole at that time of year.

Shark Encounter

SeaWorld. Sinister music and cases of shark jaws serve as the prelude to a daunting walk through a 60-foot-long, acrylic-sided and -roofed tunnel where sharks swim around and above you, providing the rare chance to see how crammed full of

▼ PACIFIC POINT PRESERVE

▲ SHARK ENCOUNTER

teeth their mouths actually are – and offering as realistic an impression as you'll get on dry land of what swimming with sharks must feel like. The aquarium is also home to other notorious predators, including barracuda, eels, and poisonous fish. If you want to get closer still, you can snorkel ($125) or scuba dive ($150) in a shark cage as part of the Sharks Deep Dive program (for reservations, call ☏1-800/432-1178 and press 4).

Wild Arctic

SeaWorld. Minimum height: 42"/107cm. Artificial snow and ice make the beluga whales, walruses, and polar bears here feel right at home. You can get to the animal viewing area quickly by walking, but if you have the time you should wait in line to board your "helicopter" for a bumpy but enjoyable flight-simulator ride through an Arctic blizzard to the remote Base Station Wild Arctic.

Anheuser-Busch Hospitality Center

SeaWorld. This small but bustling corner of the park is where free glasses of Anheuser-Busch beer are dispensed. The freebie is officially limited to two glasses per person, but this limit is not enforced with much rigor. Serving time ends at 5pm. Sign up in advance if you want to attend the informative 35-minute Budweiser Beer School (four daily), where you'll learn how beer is made, how it should be drunk, and why we should all be drinking Budweiser. The class includes several samplings.

The Waterfront

SeaWorld. The park's newest addition is a five-acre themed area re-creating a Mediterranean fishing village. Such surroundings provide a natural home for the bulk of the park's restaurants and shops, as well as being the best place to enjoy a leisurely stroll. The Waterfront's only attraction as such is the 400-foot Sky Tower, looking vaguely like Seattle's Space Needle, that soars over the lagoon and is the park's signature landmark. You can ascend the tower in rotating capsules for panoramic views over Orlando, although be prepared to pay an additional charge of $3 for the privilege.

Other SeaWorld attractions

The rest of the park is filled with more understated animal displays, including endangered sea turtles at **Turtle Point** and the incongruous presence of undeniably beautiful Clydesdale horses (the Anheuser-Busch company symbol) at the **Clydesdale Hamlet**. The area set aside for kids, **Shamu's Happy Harbor**, compares favorably with those at other theme parks, with the standard climbing nets, sandpit, inner tubes, and slides combining with slightly more challenging equipment such as remote-control boats.

Discovery Cove

Apart from the dolphin swim, there is not much else to Discovery Cove – so, unless you're a passionate lover of these gentle creatures, it may feel like a bit of a rip-off. On the other hand, since visitors are limited to no more than 1000 per day, there are no crowds. All equipment – wet suits, snorkeling gear, towels, lockers, animal-friendly sunscreen – is included in the admission price, as is lunch.

Upon entering the park, you will be given a time for your swimming-with-dolphins encounter at the **Dolphin Lagoon.** Best to immediately dispel any romantic images that the terminology inevitably evokes – the reality of the experience can be a little disappointing if you don't. Remember that this is still a theme park, and although you are now dealing with a bottlenose dolphin rather than a guy in a Mickey Mouse costume, the general approach is still the same: you must have fun at all costs.

Before going anywhere near the dolphins, you'll watch an engaging video explaining their basic characteristics and how to use hand signals to communicate with them. After this, put on your wet suit and make your way to the icy waters of the Dolphin Lagoon. For the next thirty minutes or so you and about seven other guests stand waist-deep in the water surrounding the dolphin and its trainer. You will be encouraged to stroke the docile creature, give it kisses and hugs, and finally grasp its dorsal fin for a brief swim across the lagoon.

With the dolphin swim taking a relatively small chunk out of the day, there is plenty of time (in many ways, *too* much time) to explore other parts of the park. Most of this time can be spent alternating between

sunbathing on the beach that unfolds in the center of the park and snorkeling in two pools jam-packed with fish.

In the **Coral Reef** thousands of tropical fish weave in and out of shipwrecked remains, while

▲ DOLPHIN LAGOON IN DISCOVERY COVE

▲ SNORKELING IN DISCOVERY COVE

sharks and barracuda leer at you from behind protective glass screens. You can also snorkel or wade in the shallower **Ray Lagoon**, stroking dozens of harmless Southern and Cownose rays.

While the **Tropical River and Aviary** is an attractive addition to the park, the river itself, which winds around the Coral Reef, Ray Lagoon, and past the beach, offers little more than the chance to take a leisurely swim. Passing under the river's waterfalls, either by swimming, wading, or on inflatable rings, brings you to the jungle-like Aviary, where you can stroll freely amongst over thirty species of bird, including Scarlet Ibis and toucan, all of which wander about unconstrained by cages looking for an outstretched hand full of food to perch on.

Shops

Allura's Treasure Trove
SeaWorld, The Waterfront. A doll shop where youngsters can design their own porcelain doll, choosing its race, hairstyle, eye color, and outfit – but not its price, which is predictably high.

The Oyster's Secret
SeaWorld, The Waterfront. Ask a diver to retrieve an oyster from the adjacent pearl diving lagoon, and then watch the pearl being removed and turned into the piece of jewelry of your choice.

Restaurants

Makahiki Luau Dinner Show
SeaWorld, The Waterfront, Seafire Inn ☎1-800/327-2420. Adults $42.95, children 3–9 $27.95; discounts if you book online. A captivating South Seas–style dinner show where the rhythmic music, traditional dance, and beautiful costumes all outshine the average Hawaiian and Pacific Rim food, including such dubious dishes as mahi-mahi in piña colada sauce.

Sharks Underwater Grill
SeaWorld, Shark Encounter. Strangely, this shark-themed restaurant, where you eat surrounded by sharks looking jealously at your meal, features no shark dishes on its seafood-dominated menu. Instead, the fare is salmon, shrimp, and tuna, with a few steaks thrown in for good measure. Main dishes cost around $15.

▲ THE AVIARY IN DISCOVERY COVE

▲ SHARKS UNDERWATER GRILL

Spice Mill

SeaWorld, The Waterfront. Claiming to feature "the flavors of the seven seas," this eatery overlooking the lagoon does indeed offer more exotic choices than you'll usually find at theme-park restaurants, even if the menu is restricted mainly to sandwiches costing around $8. Cajun Jambalaya, Caribbean Jerk Chicken, and Habeñero Chicken are some of the spicier sandwich fillings, offset by Beer Battered Fish.

Live shows

Clyde and Seamore Take Pirate Island

SeaWorld, Sea Lion & Otter Stadium. The storyline of this pantomime-style pirate adventure is aimed at the younger ones, but the superbly trained sea lions will impress everyone. Get there early to catch the hilarious mime artist who makes fun of arriving spectators with a blatant disregard for political correctness.

Pets Ahoy!

SeaWorld, Seaport Theater. A delightful show where cats and dogs, many of which have been rescued from local shelters, along with a variety of other more-or-less domesticated animals such as rats and pigs, perform a multitude of very cute routines.

The Shamu Adventure/Shamu Rocks America

SeaWorld, Shamu Stadium. SeaWorld's star performers are its killer whales. In The Shamu Adventure they perform tricks – like shooting their trainers high up in the air with their noses – in a huge tank, taking great pleasure in splashing the crowd with their tails (avoid the first fourteen rows if you don't want to get drenched). Shamu Rocks America follows a similar theme, this time at night to a high-tempo rock 'n' roll soundtrack.

▲ THE SHAMU ADVENTURE

International Drive and Restaurant Row

Once finished with the theme parks, the impulse of many visitors is to spend the rest of their stay experiencing the garish and much-publicized pleasures of International Drive (I-Drive for short), which, although tacky and predictable, can at least be toured on foot. Between the Belz Factory Outlet World shopping mall at its northern end and the immense Orange County Convention Center in the south, there are numerous gift shops – all claiming to be the "world's largest" – and chain restaurants and hotels, interspersed by the odd diverting attraction, from large-scale operations such as the Wet 'n' Wild water park to a few quirky museums. Just off I-Drive on Sand Lake Road, several trendy restaurants are clustered around the intersection with Dr. Philips Boulevard in an area known as Restaurant Row.

Wet 'n' Wild

6200 International Drive ☎407/351-1800 or 1-800/992-9453, ☻www.wetnwildorlando.com. Daily 10am–5pm, longer hours in summer. Adults $33.95, children 3–9 $27.95, $10 off regular prices after 2pm. Orlando's original water park has stood the test of time very well indeed and continues to offer stiff competition to Disney's Blizzard Beach and Typhoon Lagoon. Unfettered by Disney's predilection for fantastical themes, Wet 'n' Wild has put all of its energy into providing the most fun and exciting attractions possible. There are very scary, no-nonsense speed slides such as the 250-foot Der Stuka or the nearly vertical The Bomb Bay; more elaborate but slightly less intimidating flume and tube rides like the twisting Mach 5 and The Storm, which feels rather like being flushed down the toilet; and multi-person raft rides such as The Flyer, with plenty of sharp turns, and the park's brand-new Disco H2O, where your raft swirls in rhythm to 1970s disco music. Although much more compact than either of the Disney water parks, there are still some attractive areas for general lounging about and swimming, notably the Beach Club, which includes a place for picnics; and the water is heated during the colder months.

Sky Venture

6805 Visitor's Circle, across from Wet 'n' Wild ☎407/903-1150 or 1-800/759-3861, ☻www.skyventureorlando.com. Mon–Fri 2–11.30pm, Sat & Sun noon–11.30pm. Adults $38.50, children 3–12 $33.50. Fly on a column of air without a parachute in this realistic freefall skydiving simulator. The whole process lasts about an hour, and includes a basic flight training class and putting on the skydiving gear. The flight itself,

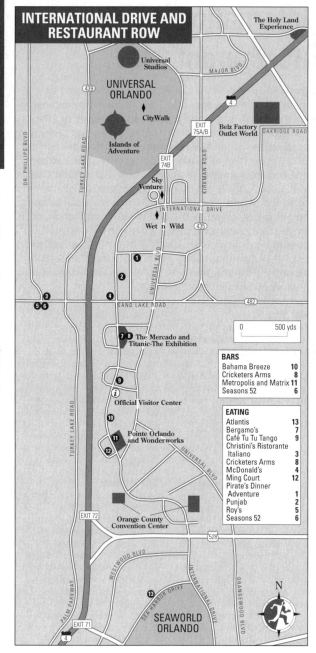

INTERNATIONAL DRIVE AND RESTAURANT ROW

The Holy Land Experience

Universal Studios

UNIVERSAL ORLANDO
(439)

CityWalk

MAJOR BLVD

4

EXIT 75A/B

Belz Factory Outlet World   OAKRIDGE ROAD

Islands of Adventure

EXIT 74B

KIRKMAN ROAD

DR PHILLIPS BLVD

TURKEY LAKE ROAD

Sky Venture

INTERNATIONAL DRIVE

Wet 'n Wild   (435)

1

2

UNIVERSAL BLVD

3

5 6   **4**   SAND LAKE ROAD   (482)

7 8 The Mercado and Titanic-The Exhibition

0	500 yds

9

i

Official Visitor Center

10

11 Pointe Orlando and Wonderworks

12

TURKEY LAKE ROAD

UNIVERSAL BLVD

EXIT 72

Orange County Convention Center

(528)

WESTWOOD BLVD

PALM PARKWAY

EXIT 71

4

INTERNATIONAL DRIVE

SEA HARBOR DRIVE

ORANGEWOOD BLVD

13

SEAWORLD ORLANDO

N

BARS
Bahama Breeze	10
Cricketers Arms	8
Metropolis and Matrix	11
Seasons 52	6

EATING
Atlantis	13
Bergamo's	7
Café Tu Tu Tango	9
Christini's Ristorante Italiano	3
Cricketers Arms	8
McDonald's	4
Ming Court	12
Pirate's Dinner Adventure	1
Punjab	2
Roy's	5
Seasons 52	6

which takes place in an indoor wind tunnel, lasts for only a couple of minutes or so, but it's an exhilarating experience. Although you can turn up on spec and get a flight, reserving in advance is preferable.

The Mercado

8445 International Drive ☎407/345-9337, ⊛ www.themercado.com.
Designed to resemble a Mediterranean village, this is one of two entertainment, shopping, and dining complexes along I-Drive that should attract a fair amount of traffic on account of its good location, but is often virtually empty. The high turnover of shops and other businesses – they seem to close as quickly as they open – is indicative of the The Mercado's rather bland character, made only fractionally more enticing by live music in the main square every night at 7.30pm, a quirky selection of shops selling magic tricks, psychic accessories, and the like, and one or two reasonably worthwhile restaurants.

Titanic – The Exhibition

The Mercado, 8445 International Drive ☎407/248-1166, ⊛ www .titanicshipofdreams.com. Daily 10am–8pm (last tour at 7pm). Adults $17.95, children 6–12 $12.95.
The one-hour guided tour of this museum recounts in good and sometimes touching detail the rise and fall of the *Titanic*, from the ship's 32-month construction through to its icy demise. Like James Cameron's film, the exhibits contrast the ship's opulent first-class accommodations and the quarantine-like conditions in which the "disease-spreading" third-class passengers lived, although most of the exhibits

▲ TITANIC – THE EXHIBITION

are props from the movie instead of artifacts from the ship itself. However, there are plenty of vintage photographs, which, along with the guide's engaging commentary, put things nicely into perspective.

Pointe Orlando

9101 International Drive ☎407/248-2838, ⊛ www.pointeorlando.com.
I-Drive's other entertainment-center-gone-haywire is a little more hip than The Mercado, featuring designer clothing stores, a multi-screen cinema, and a couple of fancy discotheques, although again businesses open and close with too much frequency to suggest that this is a compelling destination in its own right. The shops, which include AIX Armani Exchange and Victoria's Secret, offer their usual range of clothing and lingerie; the 21-screen cinema shows the latest Hollywood releases; and the two modern dance clubs (see p.122) on the top level of the complex are the pick of I-Drive's limited nightlife options.

▲ WONDERWORKS

Wonderworks

Pointe Orlando, 9067 International Drive ☎ 407/351-8800, ⊛ www .wonderworksonline.com. Daily 9am–midnight. Adults $17.95, children 4–12 $12.95. This collection of more than one hundred high-tech interactive gizmos is cleverly housed inside an upside-down creaking house. Many of the exhibits rely on simulators to re-create various exciting situations: some, such as landing the space shuttle and flying a fighter jet require a certain amount of hand-eye coordination and concentration; others such as the simulated earthquake and virtual rollercoaster let you just sit back and enjoy the ride. Quirkier contraptions include one where you get to feel what it's like to lie on a bed of 3500 nails. In the basement, meanwhile, you can shoot laser guns at one another for an extra $4.95. Perfect for teenage boys.

Orange County Convention Center

9800 International Drive ☎ 407/685-9800, ⊛ www.orlandoconvention .com. As well as being a major tourist destination, Orlando rakes in plenty of dollars from a convention business that rivals that of Las Vegas. The huge Orange County Convention Center marks the southern extremity of the pedestrian-friendly part of International Drive; beyond this, there are no sidewalks. Consisting of the West Building and the more recent, futuristic North/South Building, this is the second largest convention center in the US – and at its busiest in January, when two of the largest conventions are The International Builders' Show

▼ ORANGE COUNTY CONVENTION CENTER

▲ THE HOLY LAND EXPERIENCE

(home builders) and the PGA Merchandise Show (golf equipment; not open to the general public).

The Holy Land Experience

4655 Vineland Rd at Conroy Rd, next to the I-4 (exit 78) ☎407/367-2065 or 1-866/872-4659, ☺www.theholy landexperience.com. Open daily at various times, normally from 9am or 10am Mon–Sat and noon Sun. Adults $29.99, children 6–12 $19.99. Orlando's newest theme park opened in 2001 with the slightly controversial publicity that was bound to follow a project that deals with religious themes in the most secular of ways. This said, don't expect Noah's Ark flume rides or David vs Goliath rollercoasters. The park's primary aim is to educate – and to preach the Christian message. This is done largely through the park's architecture – such as an evocative re-building of ancient Jerusalem – various exhibits on the history of religion, including a re-creation of Christ's tomb, and the recounting of pivotal events during Jesus' lifetime in films and live performances. The topics chosen for performance are diverse in

scope and some may not be immediately recognizable to those who have only a basic knowledge of the Bible. For example, the dramatization of the building of the tabernacle by Moses likely won't resonate as much as the musical retelling of the crucifixion. The park covers a mere fifteen acres (Disney's Magic Kingdom, for example, is 107 acres) so you can easily see it in a few hours.

Shops

Belz Factory Outlet World

5401 W Oakridge Rd ☎407/352-9611, ☺www.belz.com. Shop for some incredible deals on well-known brands (including GAP, Levis, DKNY, Guess, and Calvin Klein) – or stock up on Bibles and vitamins – at Orlando's largest and most diverse factory outlet shopping mall. The mall is the last stop on the northbound I-Ride Trolley (see p.171).

The Florida Mall

8001 S Orange Blossom Trail, at Sand Lake Rd, about five miles east of I-Drive ☎407/851-6255. This

▲ ORLANDO PREMIUM OUTLETS

is Orlando's largest regular shopping center – not a factory outlet mall – so expect to pay retail prices at JC Penny, Saks Fifth Avenue, Sears, and many smaller specialty shops selling everything from clothes, jewelry, and home furnishings to cosmetics, toys, and chocolates.

Orlando Premium Outlets

8200 Vineland Ave ☎407/238-7787, ⓦwww.premiumoutlets.com. Right at the southern end of I-Drive (the last stop on the southbound I-Ride Trolley), this mall specializes in selling designer-label clothes at much reduced prices. Practically all of the major names are here, including Hugo Boss, Giorgio Armani, and Max Mara, as well as the main sports-equipment retailers.

Restaurants

Atlantis

Renaissance Orlando Resort, 6677 Sea Harbor Drive ☎407/351-5555, ⓦwww.atlantisorlando.com. A real treat for seafood lovers, this intimate upscale restaurant in the atrium of the *Renaissance Orlando Resort* is known for its rich and creamy lobster bisque ($8) – a nice prelude to several excellent fish and seafood dishes ($28–41).

Bergamo's

The Mercado, 8445 International Drive ☎407/352-3805, ⓦwww.bergamos.com. Dinner only. Authentic Italian food, from tasty antipasti ($11.95) to meatballs made with raisins, pine nuts, and spices ($15.95), served by singing waiters who perform Broadway hits, opera, and Neapolitan folk songs while you eat.

Café Tu Tu Tango

8625 International Drive ☎407/248-2222, ⓦwww.cafetututango.com. While offering original and imaginative dishes (mainly $7–10) such as mango duck quesadillas, coconut curry mussels, and alligator bites, the portions are so small that two or three are required to fill you up. All the artwork on the walls is for sale.

Christini's Ristorante Italiano

7600 Dr. Phillips Blvd ☎407/345-8770, ⓦwww.christinis.com. Dinner only. One of Orlando's best Italian restaurants, where the food, wine, and service are all impeccable, and the decor upscale and elegant. Pasta dishes (such as linguini in red or white clam sauce) cost

▲ CAFÉ TU TU TANGO

around $20, while the meat and seafood dishes, including several different veal options, are $30 and up.

Cricketers Arms

The Mercado, 8445 International Drive ☎407/354-0686. The fish and chips ($8.25–11.25), cottage pies ($8.25), and other British favorites served here make for a tasty and relatively economical choice for lunch or dinner.

McDonald's

6875 W Sand Lake Rd ☎407/351-2185, ☎www.mcfun.com. This is the largest *McDonald's* in the world – and as such no other one has as much for kids (and adults) to do than this one: video games, climbing frames, and pinball machines clutter two floors, while appetizing and good-value paninis and pasta dishes for around $6 make for an excellent and healthier alternative to the hamburgers, fries, and other usual fare on the menu.

Ming Court

9188 International Drive ☎407/351-9988, ☎www.ming-court .com. Asian cuisine of an exceptionally high standard, and made with only the freshest ingredients. Most dishes cost around $10 – good value considering the quality of the food and the beautiful decor. The meticulously prepared dim sum or a sumptuous sushi platter goes for around $20.

Pirate's Dinner Adventure

6400 Carrier Drive ☎407/248-0590 or 1-800/866-2469, ☎www .piratesdinneradventure.com. Adults $49.95, children 3–11 $29.95; discounts if you book online. Peg-leg buccaneers, scalawags, cannons,

▲ MING COURT

sword fights, and a host of stunts and songs are all part of a Broadway-style show performed on a pirate's galleon while you munch through a rather less inspiring meal of chicken in lemon-pepper sauce, beef stew, rice, and vegetables.

Punjab

7451 International Drive ☎407/352-7887, ☎www.punjabindianrestaurant .com. The flavorsome and moderately spicy curries (around $15) at this unpretentious Indian restaurant are popular with Orlando's East Asian community.

Roy's

7760 W Sand Lake Rd ☎407/352-4844, ☎www.roysrestaurant .com. Dinner only. Hawaiian chain offering an innovative island-fusion cuisine. Try the fixed-price, three-course menu ($30) for a good and relatively inexpensive sampling of what's on offer; main dishes include mahi mahi in lobster-butter sauce and miso steak grilled on a hibachi.

Seasons 52

7700 W Sand Lake Rd ☎407/354-5212, ⊛www.seasons52.com. Dinner only. All items on the menu are under 475 calories, a feat achieved by using plenty of chicken, fish, and vegetables rather than skimping on quantity. The desserts, meanwhile, come in "four-bite" portions. Most main dishes cost around $15. There are tables outside overlooking a lake, while the busy piano bar (see below) is the focal point inside.

Bars and clubs

Bahama Breeze

8849 International Drive ☎407/248-2499, ⊛www.bahamabreeze.com. Primarily a restaurant serving decent Caribbean entrees for $15–20, this place comes into its own later in the evening (particularly on Fridays and Saturdays), when crowds of thirty- and forty-somethings gather to sip cocktails, listen to live island-style music, and flirt.

Cricketers Arms

The Mercado, 8445 International Drive ☎407/354-0686. A convivial place frequented by Anglo-Saxons homesick for warm beer and soccer matches, but also with a faithful clientele of Orlando locals. There is live music nightly covering an eclectic range of genres, usually commencing at around 10pm.

Metropolis and Matrix

Pointe Orlando, 9101 International Drive ☎407/370-3700, ⊛www.metropolismatrix.com. Metropolis closed Mon–Wed, Matrix closed Mon & Tues. No expense has been spared to equip these two adjacent venues with high-tech sound systems, fancy light shows, and other eye-catching effects. As the only dance clubs on I-Drive, they often draw reasonable crowds. There is little difference between the two: the *Metropolis* is slightly more focused on dancing than the *Matrix*, where you can play billiards.

Seasons 52

7700 W Sand Lake Rd ☎407/354-5212, ⊛www.seasons52.com. This eatery on Restaurant Row is a popular place for single professionals on Wednesday, Friday, and Saturday evenings, when the piano bar does a brisk trade in cocktails, appetizers, and cheesy chat-up lines.

▲ SEASONS 52

Downtown Orlando

Orlando's sprawling and often unattractive layout is redeemed by its vibrant downtown, an area still largely ignored by visitors. City developers, on the other hand, have spent a lot of time and money in recent years on rejuvenating this part of the city. The trendy restaurants, luxurious condos, and eclectic shops, including Antique Row – a couple dozen antique stores that line Orange Avenue between Virginia Drive and Princeton Street – are very much the new face of downtown Orlando. The real draw, however, is the robust and constantly improving nightlife. Orange Avenue in particular is lined with a bewildering number of bars, lounges, and clubs of every style imaginable, all of them easily visited on foot – as is most of the downtown area.

Orange Avenue

Downtown Orlando's main thoroughfare is Orange Avenue, which continues for a few miles north towards Winter Park, with the most interesting, pedestrian-friendly stretch lying between South and Robinson streets. Trawled by lunch-seeking office workers by day, it becomes especially lively in the evenings as its numerous – and very eclectic – collection of bars, lounges, and nightclubs open for business. Sightseers should take a look at the late 1920s First National Bank (now Valencia Community College); but unfortunately the Art Deco building a few blocks north that was once McCrory's Five and Dime was one of several buildings that were torn down to make way for a shopping and entertainment complex that is currently under construction. (For another good example of Art Deco, check out the Wellborn House at The Courtyard at Lake Lucerne – see p.163.)

Lake Eola and Thornton Park
10-min walk east of Orange Avenue.

Some of the wooden homes built by Orlando's first settlers in the mid-1800s stand next to fancy high-rise condos around scenic Lake Eola. A one-mile path skirts the lake and is a popular place for jogging and dog-walking, particularly at dusk. If you'd like to get on the lake itself, you can rent

▼ FIRST NATIONAL BANK

DOWNTOWN ORLANDO

BARS, CLUBS & COMEDY

Eola Wine Company	13
Eye Spy	5
Independent Bar	8
Orlando Improv	14
Pulse	16
Rhythm and Flow Ultralounge	11
The Roxy	2
The Social	8
Southern Nights	15
Tabu	8

EATING

Dexter's of Thornton Park	6
DMAC Café	12
Hue – A Restaurant	10
Little Saigon	3
Panera Bread	4
Shari Sushi	9
The Globe	7
White Wolf Café	1

ACCOMMODATION

The Courtyard at Lake Lucerne	G
Embassy Suites	E
Eō Inn	C
Parliament House Resort	B
Travelodge	A
Veranda Bed & Breakfast	D
Westin Grand Bohemian	F

Winter Park

Harry P. Leu Gardens

Orlando Museum of Art

Loch Haven Park

Orlando Science Center

Lake Formosa

Antique Row

Lake Ivanhoe

Virginia Drive

Lake Concord

Lake Lakeview St

Marks St

Park Lake

East Colonial Drive

Hillcrest St

Concord St

Amelia St

Harwood St

DOWNTOWN ORLANDO

TD Waterhouse Centre

Lynx Central Station

Bob Carr Performing Arts Centre

Orange County Regional History Center

Livingston St

THORNTON PARK

East Robinson Street

Jefferson St

Washington St

Lake Eola

Central Boulevard

Pine St

Church St

Greyhound Bus Terminal & B

Amtrak Train Station & 16

0 — 900 yds

▲ LAKE EOLA

paddleboats that look like swans for $7 per half-hour. The several streets on the eastern side of the lake comprise Thornton Park, a trendy, upscale neighborhood. This showcase of downtown's new urbanism, full of renovated cottages, hip restaurants, and bustling coffee shops makes for a very pleasant stroll through what feels like a village within the city.

Orange County Regional History Center

65 E Central Blvd, one block east of Orange Avenue ☎407/836-8500 or 1-800/965-2030, ⊛www.thehistorycenter .org. Mon–Sat 10am–5pm, Sun noon–5pm. Adults $7, children 3–12 $3.50. This informative museum of Orlando's history is housed in the restored 1927 Orange County Courthouse on Heritage Square. For all its interactive exhibits tracing the area's history from 10,000 BC to the present day, the most intriguing displays are the old photos and re-creations of hotel lobbies, grocery stores, and the like that give a revealing glimpse of what Orlando looked and felt like before the arrival of Disney – much more the epitome of an American frontier town than the theme-park epicenter it is today.

Orlando Museum of Art

2416 N Mills Ave ☎407/896-4231, ⊛www.omart.org. Tues–Fri 10am–4pm, Sat & Sun noon–4pm. Adults $8, children 6–18 $5. Orlando's small but well-presented art museum sits in Loch Haven Park, a large lawn wedged between two lakes three miles north of downtown. The permanent collection focuses on American art from the nineteenth century to the present day – an eclectic mix of works that range from the bright and cheerful impressionist paintings of Edward Henry Potthast to an enigmatic 50-foot woodcut by African-American artist Kerry James Marshall – as well as artifacts from ancient America (2000 BC to 1521 AD) and Africa. Just as enthralling are the excellent temporary exhibitions (around ten to twelve a year) showcasing a variety of art forms by artists from both the US and abroad.

Orlando Science Center

777 E Princeton St ☎407/514-2000 or 1-888/672-4386, ⊛www .osc.org. Mon–Thurs 9am–5pm, Fri &

Sat 9am–9pm, Sun noon–5pm. Adults $14.95, children 3–11 $9.95. While virtually devoid of tourists, this all-embracing science center opposite the Orlando Museum of Art is by no means empty. It's the day-trip of choice for almost every school in the Greater Orlando area, and therefore touring this multi-level facility can be an exercise in patience. The crowds, however, are absorbed quite well over the four floors, where the plentiful interactive exhibits do a reasonable job of making astronomy, biology, energy sources, and physics more palatable subjects to formative – but wandering – minds. The main draw for adults is the CineDome, the world's largest Iwerks domed theater and Digistar II planetarium, where documentary-style films (included in the ticket price) about various natural phenomena are shown daily.

Harry P. Leu Gardens

1920 N Forest Ave, one mile east of Loch Haven Park ☎407/246-2620, ⊛www.leugardens.org. Daily 9am–5pm. Adults $5, children 3–12 $1. These lush, fifty-acre botanical gardens were purchased by a green-thumbed Orlando businessman in 1936 to show off plants collected from around the world. After seeing and sniffing the roses, azaleas, and the largest collection of camellias in the US outside of California, take a trip around Leu House (guided tours only, Aug–June daily 10am–3.30pm, included in ticket price), a late nineteenth-century farmhouse bought and lived in by Leu and his wife, now maintained in the simple but elegant style of their time and laced with family mementos.

Shops

A.J. Lillum

1913 N Orange Ave ☎407/895-6111. One of the more unique – and expensive – shops on Antique Row, containing antiques, furniture, and silver from both America and Europe.

Flo's Attic

1800 N Orange Ave ☎407/895-1800. This favorite on Orlando's Antique Row is popular as much for its quaintness as its excellent selection of wooden furniture, pottery, china, jewelry, and the like.

Fredlund Wildlife Gallery

1219 N Orange Ave ☎407/898-4544, ⊛www.fredlundwildlife.com. Closed Sun. Featuring a huge collection of paintings, prints, and sculptures of every animal imaginable, plus a few paintings of Florida landscapes. None of the works come cheap, and the best of them go for thousands of dollars.

▲ FURNITURE ON ANTIQUE ROW

Kathmandu Downtown
34 S Orange Ave. Provided you can handle the intense wafts of incense, browsing the assorted ethnic paraphernalia here makes for a good break while bar-hopping. Smokers can also stock up on natural, additive-free cigarettes. Open until 3am Monday to Saturday, till midnight Sunday.

Restaurants and cafés

Dexter's of Thornton Park
808 E Washington St ☎407/648-2777, ⓦwww.dexwine.com. This trendy yet informal eatery serves up substantial and imaginative sandwiches and salads for around $10, while the more gourmet dinner dishes such as duck confit and pan-roasted halibut are nearer $20. There is also a good wine list.

DMAC Café
39 S Magnolia Ave, at E Pine ☎407/992-1200, ⓦwww.dmacorlando.com. Closed Mon. The café of the Downtown Media Arts Center serves as a gathering place for the cinephiles who patronize the center's art-house cinema (tickets $5–7). They serve coffee and a small selection of biscuits and cakes, and there are also two computers with free Internet access.

The Globe
25 Wall St Plaza ☎407/849-9904. A good place for inexpensive Nouveau American snacks and light meals with an Asian twist, usually not costing more than around $10. The noodle bowls are a good choice, as is the chicken masala. There are some tables on the pedestrian-

▲ PANERA BREAD

only street – perfect for people watching.

Hue – A Restaurant
629 E Central Blvd ☎407/849-1800, ⓦwww.huerestaurant.com. Hip Thornton Park eatery, good for a cocktail at the bar or on the outside terrace if you can't afford the pricey food – $21–34 for main dishes, including wood-grilled meat and fish dishes with chive mashed potatoes – which is presented with plenty of style and panache, even if it does sometimes taste quite average.

Little Saigon
1106 E Colonial Drive ☎407/423-8539. One of the biggest and best of the many Vietnamese restaurants on Colonial Drive (near Mills Avenue), a couple of miles northeast of downtown. Most dishes cost around $6.

Panera Bread
227 N Eola Drive ☎407/481-1060. This great local chain offers a wonderful array of baked goods, soups, salads, and sandwiches (lunch will cost around $8), as well as the full gamut of coffee

▲ SHARI SUSHI

drinks. This is a WiFi Hotspot, which means that laptop-computer-owners with WiFi capabilities will be able to get free Internet access here.

Shari Sushi

621 E Central Blvd ☎ 407/420-9420. Closed Sun. This relatively new spot has quickly gained a good reputation for its fresh sushi, featuring conch, tuna, and the like. The decor is sleek and the clientele beautiful. Rolls (around four to six pieces or two nigiris) cost $5–9.

White Wolf Café

1829 N Orange Ave ☎ 407/895-5590. Closed Sun. Down-to-earth café on Antique Row (that also sells antiques) known for its creative sandwiches and generous salads, all for under $10.

Bars and clubs

Eola Wine Company

500 E Central Blvd ☎ 407/481-9100, ☒ www.eolawinecompany.com. Escape the noise and crowds at this refined, laid-back wine bar across from Lake Eola, where you can order two-ounce glasses of their many different wines for $2–4.

Eye Spy

12 W Washington St ☎ 407/246-1599. Accessed via an easy-to-miss-entrance around the corner from the *Independent Bar* (see below), the cozy location of this venue belies its quite raucous, but good-natured, atmosphere on the weekends.

Independent Bar

70 N Orange Ave ☎ 407/839-0457, ☒ www.independentbar.net. A dark and dingy gathering place for the alternative crowd, including plenty of Goths, this is part bar, part nightclub playing plenty of melancholic tunes from the 80s.

Pulse

1912 S Orange Ave ☎ 407/649-3888, ☒ www.pulseorlando.com. Amazing lighting effects, great sound, and a steady stream of live entertainment, including cabaret performers, drag acts, comedians, and erotic dancers, have made this a popular nightspot amongst gays and lesbians.

Rhythm and Flow Ultralounge

2 S Orange Ave ☎ 407/244-5995, ☒ www.rhythmandflow.com. Closed Sun–Tues. $5 cover after 10pm Fri & Sat. An upscale lounge with beautiful decor, including walls running with water, subtle lighting, and an excellent mix of progressive house and trance played by live DJs.

The Roxy

740 Benett Rd, just off Colonial Drive, a couple miles east of downtown ☎ 407/898-4004, ☒ www.roxyorlando .com. This large, two-level dance club is invariably packed with lovers of hip-hop, which is played on most nights.

Southern Nights

375 S Bumby Ave ☎ 407/898-0424, ☒ www.southern-nights.com.

Orlando's longest-running gay venue looks spick-and-span after recent renovations. Open seven days a week, every night has a theme – Latin, drag, 1980s, and so on – with Saturdays aimed at lesbians.

Tabu

46 N Orange Ave ☎407/648-8363, ⓦwww.tabunightclub.com. Occupying an old theater, this dance club has great potential. However, the scruffy students who like to come here for Tuesday's and Thursday's $10 "all-u-can-drink" promotions, along with the bland commercial dance music, hardly do the surroundings much justice.

Comedy

Orlando Improv

129 W Church St ☎321/281-8000, ⓦwww.orlandoimprov.com. Tickets $10–20. The Orlando franchise of the famous comedy club that started in New York in the 1960s and has since launched the careers of many top comedians. The cozy venue doubles as a restaurant, with a limited selection of main dishes, such as chicken, salmon, steak, and pasta, averaging around $15.

Live shows

Bob Carr Performing Arts Centre and TD Waterhouse Centre

▼ TABU NIGHTCLUB

▲ ORLANDO IMPROV

Less than a mile northwest of downtown, on the other side of the I-4 from the bus station. Orlando Opera ☎407/426-1700 or 1-800/33-OPERA, ⓦwww.orlandoopera.org; tickets $20–120. Orlando Ballet ☎407/426-1739, ⓦwww.orlandoballet.org; tickets $10–65. These two large performance venues host the best that Orlando has to offer in the way of performing arts and professional sports. Notable institutions such as the Orlando Opera and the Orlando Ballet stage their four or five yearly productions at the Bob Carr Performing Arts Centre, while the city's only major league professional sports team, the Orlando Magic basketball franchise, play their games at the TD Waterhouse Centre opposite. The regular basketball season runs from November to April and tickets cost $10–92 (box office ☎407/896-2442 or 1-800/4NBA-TIX).

The Social

54 N Orange Ave ☎407/246-1599, ⓦwww.orlandosocial.com. One of the most important venues in Florida for showcasing the talents of bands – both with local and national followings – playing alternative rock, grunge, and anything else that isn't mainstream. Check the website for a full list of coming attractions.

Winter Park, Eatonville, and Maitland

In sharp contrast to the institutionalized atmosphere of theme-park Orlando, three small towns to the north of the city offer their own singular character. Winter Park, about five miles northeast of downtown Orlando, is a well-to-do burg, where the combination of old wealth and new yuppie dollars has brought about an aura of unpretentious refinement, evident in its impressive array of museums. An incredibly strong sense of community pervades in nearby Eatonville, just to the east of Winter Park, which, in 1875, became the first incorporated African-American municipality in the US; it remains an important center of Black culture. While Winter Park and Eatonville are both good places to tour on foot, Maitland, directly north of Winter Park, criss-crossed by larger streets that are less pleasant to walk along, features a worthwhile art center, museum, and bird sanctuary to check out.

Park Avenue

Winter Park. Nowhere is Winter Park's upmarket status more apparent than along Park Avenue, the main north–south thoroughfare that dissects the town's small downtown. On its western side lies a shady park – the perfect foil for the chic boutiques and art galleries lining the other side of the street and for which Park Avenue has become justly famous. Along with the galleries, there is an inordinate number of beauty salons, stores selling shoes, jewelry, cigars, luxury dog accessories – in short, all that well-heeled residents could ever want. Though there are few bargains here, visitors can enjoy the window shopping or sit at one of the several street terraces, sip a coffee at one of the cafés or restaurants with outdoor seating and partake in some privileged-people watching.

Charles Hosmer Morse Museum of American Art

445 N Park Ave, Winter Park ☎ 407/645-5311, ⊛ www.morsemuseum .org. Tues–Sat 9.30am–4pm, Sun

▼ PARK AVENUE IN WINTER PARK

▲ ROLLINS COLLEGE

1–4pm; Sept–May Fri 9.30am–8pm. $3, children under 12 free. The stark white building on Park Avenue in the heart of Winter Park houses the collections of one of Winter Park's founding fathers. The major exhibits are drawn from the output of Louis Comfort Tiffany, legendary for his innovative Art Nouveau lamps and windows that furnished high-society homes around the turn of the last century. Great creativity and craftsmanship went into Tiffany's work: he molded glass while it was still soft, imbuing it with colored images of water lilies, leaves, and even strutting peacocks. The stunning leaded-glass windows are clearly the highlight of the collection, although such was the general caliber of Tiffany's work that the museum's other possessions, including paintings by Hermann Herzog and John Singer Sargent, pale in comparison.

The Cornell Fine Arts Museum

1000 Holt Ave, Winter Park ☎407/646-2526, ⊛www.rollins.edu/cfam.
On Fairbanks Avenue, which brings traffic from Loch Haven Park into Winter Park, stand the Mediterranean Revival buildings of Rollins College: the oldest college in the state, boasting a tiny but respected liberal-arts faculty. Other than its neat landscaping, the campus offers one real compelling reason to visit: the **Cornell Fine Arts Museum.** Closed for renovation at the time of writing, its permanent collection is notable for a few Italian Renaissance paintings (highlighted by Cosimo Rosselli's *Madonna and Child Enthroned*) mixed in with the staid bundle of modest nineteenth-century European and American works – plus an eccentric collection of old watch keys. The temporary exhibitions are often more contemporary and vibrant. The college also hosts the annual Bach Festival (see p.174).

Albin Polasek Museum and Sculpture Gardens

633 Osceola Ave, Winter Park ☎407/647-6294, ⊛www.polasek.org.
Sept–June Tues–Sat 10am–4pm, Sun 1–4pm. $5, children under 12 free.
The former home of Czech-born Albin Polasek is now a

MAITLAND

Lake Charity

Lake Sybolia

N LAKE SYBELLA DR

Lake Jackson

S LAKE SYBELLA DR

Maitland
Art Center

OAK AV

W VENTRIS AV.

Maitland Historical
Museum and
Telephone Museum

E HORATID AV

Audubon Center
for Birds Prey

S EAST ST

Zora Neale Hurston
National Museum
of Fine Arts

Park Lake

MAGNOLIA RD

EATONVILLE

Lake
Gem

Lake Bell

MONROE AV

RIDGEWOOD AV
LYNDALE BV
KENWOOD AV

LEGION DR
WILLIAM
DR

BENNETT AV
LOREN AV
LEWIS DR
BENJAMIN AV

PANSY

LEE ROAD

W WYMORE RD
W WYMORE RD

GAY ROAD

W WEBSTER AV

N ORLANDO AV

N DENNING DR

1

Lake Killarney

HARPER ST

A

W. MORSE BLVD.

KILLARNEY DR
STAUNTON AV
BISCAYNE AV

FAIRBANKS AV

KENTUCKY AV

OGLESBY AV

CHERRY ST
HAROLD AV
JACKSON AV

MINNESOTA AV

N ORLANDO AV

N DENNING DR

Dubsdread
Golf Club

ACCOMMODATION
Best Western
  Mount Vernon Inn **A**
Park Plaza **B**

RESTAURANTS
Blackfin   **1**
The Briarpatch   **3**
Hot Olives   **4**
Jardins du Castillon **2**
Power House   **5**

WINTER PARK, EATONVILLE, AND MAITLAND

Lake Minnehaha

Howell Branch Park

Lake Waumpi

N

Glen Haven Cemetery

Lake Maitland

Lake Osceola

Charles Hosmer Morse Museum of American Art

Scenic Boat Tour Docks

Albin Polasek Museum & Sculpture Gardens

Lake Mizell

Rollins College

Cornell Fine Arts

WINTER PARK

Lake Virginia

Lake Berry

0   1 km

showcase for his technically accomplished, realist sculpture. A woodcarver by profession, Polasek arrived penniless in the US in 1901, but, after having received a formal art training, spent much of the next fifty years winning big-money commissions, many of the profits from which have been ploughed back into this museum. The beautiful three-acre gardens are the ideal place to view the liturgical, mythical, and classical sculptures, displayed to full effect against a backdrop of colorful flowers and plants.

Zora Neale Hurston National Museum of Fine Arts

227 E Kennedy Blvd, Eatonville
☎407/647-3307. Mon–Fri 9am–4pm, Sun 2–5pm. $4 donation suggested.
Although it does have very basic rotating exhibits relating to some aspect or other of African-American life, this tiny one-room museum, named after author Zora Neale Hurston, whose family moved here in the 1890s and who used it as the setting for several of her novels, notably *Their Eyes Were Watching God*. The museum is more of a starting point for a visit to this intriguing community, which takes great pride in its pioneering past. Be sure to pick up the pamphlet *A Walking Tour of Eatonville,*

▲ VIEWS FROM SCENIC BOAT TOURS

Florida at the museum, which gives exhaustive historical explanations of every possible point of interest, all easily covered on foot in less than an hour. Of these, the Robert Hungerford Preparatory High School, the first school for African-Americans in Central Florida, and the eight-room Hurston family house have the greatest historical appeal.

Maitland Art Center

231 W Packwood Ave, Maitland
☎407/539-2181, ⊛www.maitlandartcenter.org. Mon–Fri 9am–4.30pm, Sat & Sun noon–4.30pm. Free. Comprised of 23 separate structures linked by gardens and courtyards and decorated with Aztec- and Maya-style murals, this art center's intriguing ensemble of buildings is the main reason for a visit. The permanent collection contains plenty of etchings, paintings, and sculpture by its founder, artist and

Scenic boat tours

Five minutes east of Park Avenue, the shores of attractive **Lake Osceola** are lined with the opulent homes of Winter Park's wealthiest residents. Visitors can cruise this and some of Winter Park's other lakes on pontoon boats seating eighteen for hour-long narrated **tours** leaving from the dock at 312 E Morse Blvd in Winter Park (☎407/644-4056, ⊛www.scenicboattours.com). The "scenic" part of the tour is intended to focus primarily on the rich flora and fauna – including plenty of alligators – but it often takes a backseat to gawking enviously at how the other half lives. Departures are on the hour daily 10am–4pm. $8, children 2–11 $4.

architect Jules André Smith. Smith opened the center in the 1930s as the Research Studio, inviting other American artists such as Milton Avery and Doris Lee to spend working winters there. This tradition continues with the Artists-in-Action program, which allows visitors to observe professional artists at work in their studios at most times of the year. Several painters and sculptors have claimed to have felt the presence – and artistic guidance – of Smith's ghost during their sojourns here.

▲ AUDUBON CENTER FOR BIRDS OF PREY

Maitland Historical Museum and Telephone Museum

221 W Packwood Ave, Maitland ☏407/644-2451, ⊛www .maitlandhistory.com. Thurs–Sun noon–4pm. $2. The front rooms of these combined museums host a collection of artifacts and old photographs, plus rotating exhibits, all with some bearing on Maitland life and not overly exciting unless you have a particular interest in the area. Much more fun can be had in the back room, which is filled with wonderful vintage phones, commemorating the day in 1910 when the son of a Maitland grocer installed telephones in the homes of his father's customers, enabling them to order groceries from the comfort of their armchairs. From such inauspicious beginnings, the Winter Park Telephone Company evolved.

Audubon Center for Birds of Prey

1101 Audubon Way, Maitland

☏407/644-0190, ⊛www .audubonofflorida.org. Tues–Sun 10am–4pm. $5, children 3–12 $4. The headquarters of the Florida Audubon Society is also one of the leading raptor (birds of prey) rehabilitation facilities in the Southeast, treating over seven hundred injured and orphaned birds – including ospreys, owls, hawks, eagles, falcons, and the odd vulture – a year, returning over forty percent of them back to the wild. Though the public is not allowed to see the birds intended for release actually undergoing treatment, visitors can browse the several aviaries accommodating the birds with injuries so bad that returning them to the wild would be a certain death sentence.

Shops

The Doggie Door

118 E Comstock Ave, Winter Park ☏407/644-2969, ⊛www .thedoggiedoor.com. Spoil your pooch with designer collars, beds, and bowls, or honor it by decorating your home with a multitude of dog-related bits and bobs. Even if you're not buying, pop in to get an idea of where the priorities of Winter Park's residents lie.

▲ WINTER PARK FARMERS' MARKET

Farmers' Market

At intersection of New England and New York avenues, Winter Park. Sat 7am–1pm. Shop for fresh farm produce as well as plants, flowers, and various handmade goods at this weekly market, located in a former train station.

Scott Laurent Galleries

348 N Park Ave, Winter Park ☎407/629-1488. One of Park Avenue's most absorbing galleries, full of miscellaneous *objets d'art*, including some wonderfully colorful glasswork and an array of old- and new-style lamps.

Shou'Ture

339 S Park Ave, Winter Park ☎407/647-9372, ⊛www.shouture .com. The designer shoes here are definitely on the pricey

▼ SHOU'TURE

side, but the blow is softened somewhat by free pedicures and manicures with purchases and a daily Champagne Happy Hour.

Timothy's Gallery

236 N Park Ave, Winter Park ☎407/629-0707, ⊛www .timothysgallery.com. Timothy's features the work of diverse American artists, from elegantly designed jewelry, silk jackets, and scarves, to rather bizarre sculptures in clay and metal.

Restaurants

Blackfin

460 N Orlando Ave, Winter Park ☎407/691-4653. A mile or so west of downtown Winter Park in the Winter Park Village shopping complex, this restaurant prides itself on having the freshest seafood, with most main dishes costing $15–20.

The Briarpatch

252 N Park Ave, Winter Park ☎407/628-8651. Although it mainly serves rather ordinary and overpriced sandwiches (around $10), *The Briarpatch* is reputed for its huge – and again, expensive – slices of multi-flavored cakes. This is also a great place to sip a coffee, either inside or at tables on Park Avenue.

Hot Olives

463 W New England Ave, Winter Park ☎407/629-1030. The only olives on the menu are the "spicy fried" ones that come as a starter. Otherwise, the dishes here are simple with a gourmet touch, such as the shrimp in a vodka cream sauce, and for the most part cost $15–20. Closed Sun.

Jardins du Castillon

348 N Park Ave, Winter Park

▲ JARDINS DU CASTILLON

☎407/644-7229. Tucked away in a small gallery of shops, this intimate French restaurant offers three excellent meat and fish dishes for dinner ($17–28). They serve less spectacular crêpes for lunch, as well as some superb desserts. Closed Sun eve & Mon.

Power House

109–111 E Lyman Ave, Winter Park ☎407/645-3616. The place for an uncomplicated Middle Eastern–style sandwich, a tasty soup, or a vitamin-packed fruit juice, all at economical prices (around $5 for most sandwiches).

South of Orlando

The area south of Orlando, stretching fifteen miles or so south and east from Walt Disney World, appears at first glance to offer the same rows of strip malls, chain restaurants, and fly-by-night tourist attractions found elsewhere in the city. Indeed, the urban scenery in these parts, especially along US-192, is even uglier than usual. Fortunately, the rural and attractive scenery south of the highway features several attractions – usually based in some way on animals. The anomaly here is Celebration, a squeaky-clean town that is the "living" extension of the Disney theme parks just to the north. With this exception, however, the rest of the area is marked by a rustic atmosphere as genuine as it is unexpected, a welcome contrast to the more hectic pace of Orlando.

Gatorland

1401 S Orange Blossom Trail ☎407/855-5496 or 1-800/393-5297, ⓦwww.gatorland.com. Daily 9am–5pm. $21.25, children 3–12 $10.60. Opened in 1949 when tourists began visiting the state in significant numbers, Gatorland showcases the region's most famous animal: the alligator. The park's residents also include crocodiles (whose noses are more pointed than alligators'), llamas, emus, and a Black Bear called Judy. For most of the day the gators and crocs lie motionless, refusing to budge even for the cold hot-dogs thrown at them by visitors,

but for the twice-daily Gator Jumparoo Show they use their powerful tail muscles to leap from the water to snap up whole chickens held out on sticks. In Jungle Crocs of the World, smaller crocodiles compete with just as much alacrity for smaller morsels of chicken; the Gator Wrestlin' Show is self-explanatory; while the Up-Close Encounters Show involves sharing assorted creepy-crawlies with the most terrified-looking members of the audience. The entire park, including all of the shows, can easily be seen in half a day.

Celebration

ⓦwww.celebrationfl.com. Created by Disney, this town, nestled between Kissimmee and the theme parks, opened in 1996. The design attempts to capture the American ideal of community: old-fashioned exteriors, homes close to the road so neighbors are more likely to interact, and a congenial downtown area beside a tranquil

▲ RURAL FARMLAND ALONG US-192

lake. Famous architects were brought in to design some of downtown's buildings – check out Cesar Pelli's 1950s-style cinema – and the first 350 home sites sold out before a single model was even complete. Enthusiasts applaud Celebration's friendly small-town feeling, where town events are well attended and children can walk carefree to school, all without being a gated community. Detractors use words such as "contrived" and "sterile" to describe the atmosphere. Like or loathe the concept, Celebration is an undeniably pleasant place to spend a few hours. There are several good restaurants and walking around the virtually traffic-free streets is as relaxed as it gets in and around Orlando. The lake can be enjoyed to its fullest from the quiet terrace at the charming *Celebration Hotel* (see p.164).

▲ CELEBRATION

Old Town

5770 W Irlo Bronson Memorial Hwy, Mile Marker #9, Kissimmee ☎407/396-4888 or 1-800/843-4202, ⊛www.old-town.com. Daily 10am–11pm. Free entry, buy individual tickets for each ride or an all-day pass for $15 Mon–Thurs or $20 Fri–Sun. This throwback to a traditional fairground comes complete with a Ferris wheel, go-kart track, bumper cars, merry-go-round, spinning teacups, and a rickety-looking rollercoaster – all charmingly quaint when compared with

the high-tech attractions elsewhere in Orlando. There are also 75 shops to browse, from the interestingly quirky to downright tacky (see "Shops," p.143). The best time to visit Old Town is on Saturday night all year round, when, at 8.30pm, the hundreds of classic cars that started arriving early in the afternoon are paraded up and down the streets in what is the largest weekly classic-car cruise in the US.

Kissimmee and Lake Tohopekaliga

Once the hub of Florida's important cattle industry, Kissimmee retains to this day its cowboy feel. Its most compelling feature is three-mile-long Lakeshore Boulevard, which offers a good look at

US-192

Also known as **Irlo Bronson Memorial Highway**, this unappealing road is the main east–west corridor south of Orlando, running past a good many of the sights mentioned in this chapter. It uses a system of **Mile Markers**: numbered boards roughly one mile apart along either side of the road that serve as reference points – Old Town, for example, is at Mile Marker #9, and the turn-off for World Drive (for Walt Disney World) is at Mile Marker #7.

▲ Walt Disney World

SOUTH OF ORLANDO

La Quinta Inn Lakeside
(Orange Blossom Balloons) **4**

WORLD DRIVE

BUENA VISTA DRIVE

VINELAND AVE

(192)

6

5

OLD LAKE WILSON ROAD

A World of Orchids

7

8 **❶** **10**

IRLO BRONSON MEMORIAL HWY

9

Old Town Kissimmee

CENTRAL FLORIDA GREENEWAY

27

4

CELEBRATION BLVD

FRONT ST

5 **4** **3**

Celebration Town

Green Meadows Petting Farm

532

S. ORANGE BLOSSOM TRAIL

RESTAURANTS

Arabian Nights Dinner Show	1
Café d'Antonio	4
Catch Pen Saloon	6
Celebration Town Tavern	5
Columbia	3
Medieval Times Dinner & Tournament	2
Susan's Courtside Café	7

4 - - Mile Markers

▼ Tampa

pretty **Lake Tohopekaliga**, headwaters to the Everglades and home to many of Florida's native birds. Others may prefer an airboat ride (see opposite).

The only other thing worth seeing here stands on the corner of Monument Avenue and Johnston Street. The eccentric Monument of States, erected in 1943 to honor the former president of the local All-States Tourist Club, is a forty-foot obelisk comprising garishly painted concrete blocks adorned with pieces of stone and fossil representing all of the American states and twenty foreign countries.

Reptile World Serpentarium

5705 E Irlo Bronson Memorial Hwy, St Cloud ☎407/892-6905. Oct–Aug Tues–Sun 9am–5.30pm. $5.75, children 6–17 $4.75, children 3–5 $3.75. George VanHorn has been handling snakes for years, and the stub at the end of one of his fingers is testament to the occupational hazards of extracting snake venom for sale to anti-venom research laboratories. The fascinating extraction process can be viewed twice daily at 12.15pm and 3.15pm, featuring George, his wife, and several moody vipers, rattlesnakes, and cobras. The show takes place behind a glass screen, but you can still see clearly as the poison drips into vials, sometimes in veritable torrents. The remainder of the attraction consists of a caged collection of venomous and non-venomous snakes from around the world and can be perused quickly.

▼ CLASSIC-CAR CRUISE IN OLD TOWN

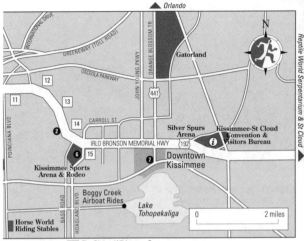

Kissimmee Sports Arena & Rodeo

1010 Suhl's Lane, off Hoagland Blvd ☏407/933-0020, ⊛www.ksarodeo .com. Fri 8pm; closed Dec. \$18, children under 12 \$9. Although nothing like Kissimmee's Silver Spurs Rodeo (see p.175) in terms of size and quality, this weekly gathering of local cowboys affords a glimpse of the hokey place that this must have been before Disney's arrival. Certain concessions to the tourists have been made, but if you can sit through the steady stream of bad jokes and endure the moment when packs of kids from the audience are invited to chase terrified calves around the arena, you will be treated to a reasonably authentic rodeo. After the over-rehearsed shows at the theme parks, the unpredictability of irate bulls is an unexpected treat, and the bull riding and subsequent efforts to get the beasts into their pens is by far the main attraction. The show lasts until around 10.30pm, but further entetainment can be found at the *Catch Pen Saloon* (see p.145) behind the grandstand.

Boggy Creek Airboat Rides

Although lasting just thirty rather noisy minutes, an **airboat ride on Lake Tohopekaliga** (☏407/344-9550, ⊛www.bcairboats.com. Oct–May daily 9am–5pm; June–Sept Mon–Fri 9am–5pm. \$18.95, children 3–12 \$14.95) is the ideal way to glimpse some of the wildlife present in these parts. The boats skid across the water at speeds of up to 45mph, hardly approaching the animals by stealth. Nevertheless, you stand a good chance of spotting an alligator or two snoozing among the reeds and, high up in the cypress trees on the riverbanks, bald eagles. To get to the departure point for rides, go south from the intersection of Poinciana Boulevard and US-192 (Mile Marker #11) for about eighteen miles until you reach Southport Park. One-hour night tours (when alligators are at their most active) are also offered (March–Oct only; \$29.95, children 3–12 \$24.95).

▲ LAKE TOHOPEKALIGA

Green Meadows Petting Farm

1368 S Poinciana Blvd ☎407/846-0770, ✆www.greenmeadowsfarm.com. Daily 9.30am–4pm. $19. This petting zoo goes several steps further than the various opportunities Disney provides for children to play with animals. For a start, the country setting is considerably more rural and peaceful than any theme park could hope to be. The price of admission includes a two-hour guided tour, taking in pigs, cows, chickens, turkeys, donkeys, and other farmyard animals, where the reasonably informative commentary takes a definite backseat to hands-on experience, from simple stroking and petting to the full-blown milking of a cow. Kids can also enjoy pony and tractor rides.

Horse World Riding Stables

3705 S Poinciana Blvd, Kissimmee ☎407/847-4343, ✆www.horseworldstables.com. Daily 9am–5pm. $39–69. The horses may be only slightly more animated than an Audio-Animatronics figure, but riding them along the nature trails around these stables is a pleasant way to get away from the theme-park hustle and bustle. There are three different rides to choose from, lasting from 45 to 90 minutes. The Nature Trail Ride and the Intermediate Trail Ride are very tame and suitable for the whole family; the Advanced Trail Ride involves some cantering and is by reservation only.

The Disney Wilderness Preserve

2700 Scrub Jay Trail, Kissimmee ☎407/935-0002. Daily 9am–5pm. $3, children 6–17 $2. For Disney to continue developing its Central Florida land holdings, it was legally required to mitigate the impact that such development would have on the environment

▼ ALLIGATOR REPTILE WORLD SERPENTARIUM

Orange Blossom Balloons

To appreciate what a rural landscape this really is, full of lakes, swamps, and forests, those who can afford it can take a one-hour hot-air balloon ride over the Central Florida countryside (for reservations ☎407/239-7677, ⊛www .orangeblossomballoons.com. $175, children 10–15 $95).

The exact flight path is dependent on the winds (the actual launch site is also determined by wind direction), but every effort is made to fly as close as possible to Disney. Upon landing you drink a Champagne toast, then head back for a buffet breakfast. Rendezvous daily at 6am at *La Quinta Inn Lakeside*, 7769 W Irlo Bronson Memorial Hwy.

by creating a large, ecologically significant project nearby. This obligation was fulfilled in 1992 when Disney acquired 8500 acres of a former ranch twelve miles southwest of Kissimmee and handed it over to The Nature Conservancy.

So, despite bearing the Disney name, this place has nothing to do with theme parks, yet it is, in fact, a wonderfully peaceful place, where the only construction has been a three-mile walking trail with a couple of benches and tables for picnics. Wetlands are scattered throughout the preserve, homes to diverse populations of wading birds, including endangered Florida sandhill cranes and woodstorks.

Shops

Instant Ancestors (Old Town Portrait Gallery)

5770 W Irlo Bronson Memorial Hwy, Old Town ☎407/892-6953. Have your face inserted into realistic old-fashioned portraits of cowboys, saloon girls, Victorian families, Civil War generals, and the like.

Lanier's Historic Downtown Marketplace

108 Broadway Ave, downtown Kissimmee ☎407/933-5679, ⊛www .laniersantiques.com. Space in this large, chaotically organized antique store is rented out to different vendors, which ensures an eclectic selection, including some colorful cow figurines. Closed Sun.

Makinson Hardware Store

308 Broadway Ave, downtown Kissimmee ☎407/847-2100. Opened in 1884, Florida's oldest operating hardware store has long since been surpassed by the big chains – but does do a fine line in plastic models of horses and cattle. Closed Sun.

Old Town Leather

5770 W Irlo Bronson Memorial Hwy, Old Town ☎407/396-1356, ⊛www .oldtownleather.com. The place for all things leather: biker jackets, wallets, cowboy hats, and belts, of which there is a particularly large selection.

▲ GREEN MEADOWS PETTING FARM

▲ COLUMBIA RESTAURANT

A World of Orchids

2501 Old Lake Wilson Rd, Kissimmee ☎407/369-1887, ⓦwww .aworldoforchids.com. Much of the fun behind this vast conservatory crammed with thousands of rare and beautiful orchids from all over the world derives from just strolling around as you would a botanical garden. All of the plants are for sale, along with other garden accessories. Closed Mon.

Restaurants and cafés

Arabian Nights Dinner Show

6225 W Irlo Bronson Hwy, Kissimmee ☎407/239-9223 or 1-800/553-6116, ⓦwww.arabian-nights.com. $47, children 3–11 $29; discounts if you book online. Eat quite good prime rib dinners while taking in a show made memorable not by the ham acting and flimsy storyline, but by the seventy-strong cast of strikingly beautiful horses, including the Black Stallion, a gift of Walter Farley, creator of the eponymous fictional horse.

Café d'Antonio

691 Front St, Celebration ☎407/566-2233. The good Italian food here includes plenty of meat dishes (mainly beef and veal for $20–35, plus some chicken offerings for around $15), along with some tempting pasta creations ($10–18). The atmosphere, however, may be a bit on the stuffy side.

Celebration Town Tavern

721 Front St, Celebration ☎407/566-2526. The Bostonian owners have made New England seafood (costing $13–30) the house specialty here, although the barbecue baby back ribs ($16.95) are possibly the best thing on the menu. From 10pm to 2am you can order light meals at the bar – convenient given the relatively early closing hours of Celebration's other restaurants.

Columbia

649 Front St, Celebration ☎407/566-1505, ⓦwww.columbiarestaurant .com. The elegant dining room looks like something straight out of a luxurious Iberian villa and the Spanish food, notably

the paella, is of an appropriately high standard. Main courses are $16 and up and there is live Spanish folk music on Friday evenings.

Medieval Times Dinner & Tournament

4510 W Irlo Bronson Hwy, Kissimmee ☎407/396-2900 or 1-888/935-6878, ⓦwww.medievaltimes.com. $48.95, children 3–11 $32.95; discounts if you book online. Knights joust on Andalusian stallions and display fine stage fighting skills as wenches serve a simple but hearty feast of roast chicken and spare ribs inside a replica eleventh-century castle.

Sherlock's of Celebration

715 Bloom St, Celebration ☎407/566-1866, ⓦwww.sherlocksofcelebration .com. An English-style teahouse (with delicious slices of cake for around $5) that also sells various fine wines by the bottle to take away.

Susan's Courtside Café

18 S Orlando Ave, downtown Kissimmee ☎407/518-1150. One of a handful of lunchtime eateries catering to the office workers in downtown Kissimmee, this one has good sandwiches and home-made pizza for around $7 and up. Lunch only, closed Sun.

Bars

Catch Pen Saloon

Kissimmee Sports Arena & Rodeo, 1010 Suhl's Lane, off Hoagland Blvd. Plenty of cold beer (though not much else) is served here after the rodeo (see p.141), and the presence of a good Country 'n' Western band makes this a popular place for a night out among locals. Fridays only; closed Dec.

Celebration Town Tavern

721 Front St, Celebration ☎407/566-2526. Open until 2am, long after the rest of Celebration has closed down for the night, the bar area of this restaurant is a great place to strike up conversations with tourists and locals alike.

▲ COUNTRY MUSIC AT THE KISSIMMEE SPORTS ARENA & RODEO

Day-trips

While there are certainly more than enough things to do in Orlando and its parks to fill a one- and even a two-week stay, other points of interest – and the beach – are never too far away. This chapter suggests a handful of possible day-trips, none more than a two-hour drive from the city. Besides some well-known and well-trod tourist destinations such as Tampa's Busch Gardens and the Kennedy Space Center on the east coast, there are a few quirky, offbeat places that reveal sides of Central Florida not immediately apparent to the casual visitor.

Busch Gardens

3000 E Busch Blvd, Tampa. Two miles east of I-275 or two miles west of I-75, exit 51 coming from the north or exit 265 coming from the south. A theme park on the scale of those at Disney, Universal, and SeaWorld, Tampa's Busch Gardens is the most obvious day-trip from Orlando, largely because park entrance is included in the Orlando FlexTicket (for more details on visiting Busch Gardens, see "Theme park practicalities" in Essentials). That said, the park will certainly appeal to animal lovers and contains some superb thrill rides that compare very favorably with those on offer in Orlando.

Busch Gardens, which opened in 1959 as a brewery (Anheuser-Busch is the park's owner), was developed into a park six years later, taking Africa as its theme. The park is divided into several areas, the biggest single section being the eighty-acre **Serengeti Plain**. It's roamed by giraffes, buffaloes, zebras, antelopes, black and white rhino, and elephants, and is the closest the place gets to showing anything genuinely African; look down on the beasts from the Skyride cable car or get a closer view from the pseudo-steam train that traverses the park (no extra charge for either mode of transport). The **Myombe Reserve**, with its collection of chimps and gorillas kept in a tropical environment complete with waterfall and even mist, is also a good attempt to re-create an African feel and is worth a look. Although the other areas bear names such as Morocco, Egypt, Timbuktu, and Congo, their links with the continent are more tenuous. Rides rather than animals

▲ THE VILLAGES

CENTRAL FLORIDA

Jacksonville

Ormond Beach

Daytona Beach

Barberville

DeLeon Springs

LAKE WOODRUFF NATIONAL WILDLIFE REFUGE

Deland

Cassadaga

The Villages

HONTOON ISLAND STATE PARK

BLUE SPRING STATE PARK

Leesburg

Mount Dora

Sanford

Lake Apopka

Orlando

Titusville

Walt Disney World

Kennedy Space Center

Celebration

Kissimmee

Polk City

Davenport

Lake Tohopekaliga

FLORIDA'S TURNPIKE

Haines City

Winter Haven

Bartow

Lake Wales

Lake Kissimmee

OCALA NATIONAL FOREST

Lake George

Lake Oklawaha

Tallahassee

Tampa

Busch Gardens & Tampa

0   10 miles

N

predominate here. There are two flume rides in Stanleyville and an even wetter raft ride in Congo, plus a small rollercoaster for children in Timbuktu. These all pale in comparison with the park's stellar collection of amazing thrill rides. The most recent addition is **Sheikra** in Stanleyville, with its terrifying 200-foot, 90-degree dive, joining Congo's **Kumba**, full of high-speed plunges and loop-the-loops, Morocco's **Gwazi**, a giant wooden coaster,

and Egypt's **Montu**, a very high, inverted coaster that leaves your feet dangling precariously in mid-air – possibly the most frightening of them all. After all this, retire to the Hospitality House and enjoy two free cups of various Anheuser-Busch beers.

The Villages

1100 Main St, The Villages ☎352/753-2270 or 1-800/346-4556, ⊛www.thevillages.com. Central Florida is dotted with communities, occasionally described as "country clubs," where seniors can live out their remaining years in peace – and sometimes considerable luxury. One such community, The Villages, sprawling on either side of US-27 roughly halfway between the towns of Leesburg and Ocala, is among the fastest growing in the US; in these parts, The Villages is considered a town in its own right. Thanks to seven eighteen-hole golf courses (all open to the public) and a multitude of shops, restaurants, and services, including a fully equipped hospital, residents rarely have the need – or inclination – to venture beyond the gates. Should you wish to sample Floridian retirement living on its grandest scale, you can do so for surprisingly little. A six-night stay at a fully furnished guest villa costs from $600 to $900; and this includes 300 to 450 "Village dollars," which can be spent on most goods and services in the community.

Mount Dora

US-441 about 40 miles northwest from Orlando. A Victorian-era Florida village set on a pristine lake, Mount Dora is all picket fences, wrought-iron balconies, and fancy wood-trimmed buildings. The town is quaint to the point of being a little nauseating after a couple of hours, yet this is all you need to visit compact Mount Dora on foot – browsing the several fine antique shops and taking tea and scones are fun distractions. If you don't feel like walking, the Mount Dora Trolley offers narrated historic and scenic tours of the town's parks, monuments, and significant buildings (including some of the main antique stores), as well as a good look at the lake. It lasts about an hour and leaves from next to the *Lakeside Inn* (Mon–Fri 11am, noon, 1pm & 2pm, with an additional tour at 3pm on Sat; $9.95, children $7; ☎352/406-8888).

Cassadaga

Just east of I-4 (exit 114), fifteen miles north of Sanford and about 35 miles from Orlando. A village deep in the forest populated by spiritualists is just about as far from the classic Orlando vacation experience that you can get. Cassadaga has existed

▲ HONTOON ISLAND STATE PARK

▲ BLUE SPRING STATE PARK

since 1875, when a young New Yorker bought 35 acres of land after being told during a séance that one day he would be instrumental in founding a spiritualist community.

There are several spiritual centers in the village offering services encompassing everything from psychic advice, palm and tarot readings, interpretations of astrological charts, communication with the spiritual world through a medium, and recollection of memories from past lives through hypnosis. Prices vary little from center to center: $50 for 30 minutes, $75 for 45 minutes, and $100 for an hour are the usual rates. The Cassadaga Spiritualist Camp (☎386/228-2880, ⓦwww .cassadaga.org), in the Andrew Jackson Davis Building, on the corner of Route 4139 (Cassadaga Road) and Stevens Street, takes a more all-embracing approach than the other centers, offering regular seminars and lectures covering topics ranging from UFO cover-ups to out-of-body traveling, along with weekly – presumably non-psychic – bingo evenings. The Universal Centre of Cassadaga, across the street at

460 Cassadaga Rd (☎386/228-3190, ⓦwww.universalcentre .net), will give readings over the telephone; while the Spiritual Center at *The Cassadaga Hotel*, 355 Cassadaga Rd (☎386/228-2323, ⓦwww.cassadagahotel .com; rooms from $50), uses hypnosis to help you lose weight. Other than the spiritualist centers, there are no sights in Cassadaga, but with their *Blair Witch Project*–style location they imbue the town with a captivatingly surreal and slightly eerie atmosphere.

Blue Spring State Park

2100 W French Ave, Orange City
☎386/775-3663. Daily 8am–sunset.
Cars $5, pedestrians and cyclists $1.
The year-round 72°F (22°C) waters at Blue Spring State Park, thirty miles or so north of Orlando – take I-4 to exit 114 and then go south on US-17/92 for a couple of miles – attract manatees between mid-November and mid-March. Affectionately known as "sea cows," these best-loved of Florida's endangered animals swim here from the cooler waters of the St Johns River, and the colder it is there the

▲ DAYTONA BEACH

more manatees you'll see here. Several observation platforms have been constructed for viewing purposes, and although swimming with the manatees is not permitted, you can swim, snorkel, and scuba dive in the springs when there are none present. For a modest historical diversion, check out Thursby House, a large frame dwelling built by pioneer settlers in 1872. Blue Spring Park can get quite crowded, especially at weekends, so consider a trip across the St Johns River to the much quieter, uninhabited **Hontoon Island State Park** (☎386/326-3521), a verdant dollop of wooded land, offering plenty of shade for picnicking, set within very flat and swampy terrain. Without a private boat, Hontoon Island is reachable only by the free ferry (daily 8am to an hour before sunset) from a landing stage off Route 44, six miles west of the town of Deland.

If you wish to stay the night in Blue Spring State Park, there's a $20-a-night campground and air-conditioned cabins for $80 that sleep up to four people. In Hontoon Island State Park, you can choose from basic camping sites for $12 a night or rustic cabins costing $25 for four people or $30 for six people.

Daytona Beach

Fifty miles northeast of Orlando along I-4. Though better known for its annual motorbike and NASCAR racing events (see p.174), Daytona Beach is the most feasible beach trip within spitting distance of Orlando. Once a renowned hot-spot for college kids on Spring Break, the town has made a conscious effort in recent years to distance itself from such shenanigans. However, the bikers and racecar enthusiasts who have largely taken the place of the students have hardly made this spot the epitome of refinement. The pervading atmosphere is one of a somewhat tacky seaside town, full of amusement arcades, T-shirt shops, and jet-ski rides.

The beach, however, is the main reason for a visit: a wide, twenty-mile stretch of light brown sand. Unusually for Florida, you are allowed to drive your car and park it on designated stretches of the beach ($5 from February to November). The busiest section of the beach is around the pier at the end of Main Street (no cars are allowed on the beach in the immediate vicinity of the pier); while three miles to the north along the seafront Atlantic Avenue, **Ormond Beach** (also no cars on the beach) is calmer and more upscale.

Kennedy Space Center

Fifty miles east of Orlando along routes 538 (Beeline Expressway) or 50. Occupying a flat, marshy island which doubles, paradoxically, as a wildlife refuge, the center is a hugely (and justifiably) popular tourist attraction – as well as, of course, being the nucleus of the US space program. The departure point of all visits is the **KSC Visitor Complex** (daily 9am–6pm), a museum dedicated to everything space-related. There are opportunities here to take part in a light-hearted interactive mission to Mars, inspect spacesuits and actual mission capsules, and examine old rockets in the nearby **Rocket Garden**. The highlight, however, is the **IMAX theater**, where two films convey quite effectively many of the sensations of space travel on five-story screens using footage from actual missions.

The second part of the visit consists of the **Kennedy Space Center Tour**. A bus (daily 10am–2.50pm) leaves from the KSC Visitor Complex for the Vehicle Assembly Building, a gargantuan structure inside which Space Shuttles are assembled and loaded with payloads (equipment carried by spacecraft) before being rolled along the huge tracks of the "crawlerway" towards the launch pad. Unfortunately, access to the VAB is prohibited, and the bus continues swiftly on to a vantage-point from which you can gaze at the **launch pad**, which, if a Space Shuttle is not already in place ready for take-off (a rarity these days), is no more interesting than any other large pile of scaffolding. The remainder of the tour includes an inspection of a Saturn V rocket, which took the first Apollo mission into space, and an impressive simulated Apollo countdown and take-off.

If you want to witness a **real-life launch**, call ☎321/449-4444 or visit ⊛www.kennedyspacecenter.com for dates and times, as well as the various launch-viewing packages on offer (which sell out very quickly). There is a special restricted viewing area six miles away, although the magnitude of the blast is awesome enough from anywhere within a forty-mile radius. Nighttime launches are especially spectacular.

▼ KENNEDY SPACE CENTER

Kennedy Space Center practicalities

Coming from Orlando **on Route 538**, take Route 407 until it reaches Route 405, then follow the signs for the Kennedy Space Center. Coming from Orlando **on Route 50**, take the Route 405 exit (the first one after going under the I-95), then follow the signs.

Standard **admission** includes access to the KSC Visitor Complex, the IMAX movies, and the Kennedy Space Center Tour ($30, children 3–11 $20). The Maximum Access Badge includes all of above, plus access to the Astronaut Hall of Fame just down the road in Titusville ($37, children 3–11 $27).

In addition to the Kennedy Space Center Tour, the **NASA Up-close Tour** gives an even closer look at the launch pad and takes you to a facility that makes components for the International Space Station; and the **Cape Canaveral: Then & Now Tour** visits the now-retired launch sites of the Mercury, Gemini, and Apollo programs (both tours: $22, children 3–11 $16; reservations recommended).

Shops

Accent China

585 Seneca Oaks Circle, Mount Dora ☎352/385-9155, ⊛www.accentchina .com. Very tasteful Chinese furniture is featured here, from ornate, old-fashioned wardrobes and bookcases to more modern creations such as chests for storing CDs, and TV cabinets.

Cassadaga Spiritualist Camp Bookstore

112 Stevens St, Cassadaga ☎386/228-2880, ⊛www.cassadaga.org. Browse through the large selection of books about spiritualism and metaphysics, or pick up a soothing CD to help with your meditation.

Double Creek Pottery

430 N Donnelly St, Mount Dora ☎352/735-5579. Fine handmade ceramics and pottery decorated with various designs, usually in soft pastel colors.

Flea World

4311 Orlando Ave, Sanford ☎407/330-1792, ⊛www.fleaworld.com. Fri–Sun 9am–6pm. This huge warehouse fifteen miles north of Orlando on US-17/92 accommodates over 1700 vendors selling everything from computer equipment to wine racks. There's a lot of junk, so you'll have to be patient to find that hidden treasure.

Renningers Antique Center

20651 US-441, just east of Mount Dora ☎352/383-8393 or 1-800/522-3555, ⊛www.renningersflorida.com. Sat & Sun 9am–5pm. A great one-stop-shop for antique hunters, this weekend market is attended by most of the area's antique shops. In addition to buying, various repair and restoration services are offered. There is an extra big market with nearly twice the number of dealers on the third weekend of every month (except December).

Restaurants and cafés

Crown Colony House Restaurant

Busch Gardens, Tampa. The park's best restaurant has large glass windows giving a nice view of the animals in the Serengeti Plain. The food is pretty standard: a roughly equal balance of seafood and meat dishes for $15–20, with a few fried items thrown in for the kids.

The Goblin Market

311b N Donnelly St, Mount Dora ☎352/735-0059. An intimate and romantic restaurant hidden down a quiet side-street, with a candle-lit dining room, outside patio, and gourmet meals such as stuffed pork loin and mushroom chicken ragout in the $15–20 price range.

Main Street Pier & Restaurant

1200 Main St, at the pier, Daytona Beach ☎386/238-1212. A long-standing favorite where you can enjoy generous portions of fried clams, hot or cold shrimp, or burgers, while watching the goings-on around the pier. Most main courses run from $10 to $15.

The Windsor Rose Tea Room

144 Fourth Ave, Mount Dora ☎352/735-2551. A decent spread of tea and scones will set you back around $20, while for the hungrier, hearty English delicacies, such as Cornish pasties and Scotch eggs, are also available.

▲ WINDSOR ROSE TEA ROOM

Accommodation

Hotels, motels, and B&Bs

Orlando has thousands of rooms in a wide range of establishments, from luxury resorts, such as those found at Walt Disney World and Universal Orlando, to the numerous chain hotels on or near International Drive, dotted around Disney property in an area called Lake Buena Vista, and along US-192 to the south of Orlando. Add to this a few privately owned hotels and bed and breakfasts, situated mainly in downtown Orlando, and the choice is quite varied.

In a sprawling city like Orlando, your stay will be guided as much by location as by price. If you don't have your own transport, think about staying along International Drive or in downtown Orlando, both areas with good local bus connections. The resorts at Disney and Universal, both of which offer free transportation between the resorts and the parks, will also negate the need for a car provided you are planning a Disney- or Universal-only vacation. Most of the Lake Buena Vista and US-192 hotels offer free shuttles to Disney, but getting anywhere else will require your own transport.

The prices at the Disney and Universal resorts are generally the highest you'll pay, with some of the fancier places demanding in excess of $300 per night, but in most cases you really do get what you pay for – well-appointed rooms, lush, landscaped grounds, several swimming pools, fine dining, and impeccable service. The hotels in Lake Buena Vista, International Drive, and downtown Orlando tend to be mid-range, usually not costing more than $150. You'll find the budget-priced motels lining US-192, where you can get a room for around $50 per night.

Booking a room

You can reserve a room at virtually all Orlando hotels on either the Internet or by telephone (many establishments have toll-free numbers for bookings made within the US); the central reservation lines for Disney and Universal resorts can be found in the boxes on p.158 & p.162. Book well in advance if you want to stay at a Disney or Universal resort during the busy summer months or around Easter, while in January a few huge conventions fill up the hotels near the Orange County Convention Center and elsewhere in the vicinity of International Drive. Rooms are increasingly easier to find in Lake Buena Vista, downtown Orlando, and finally along US-192, where you can get a room at pretty much any time of the year.

The prices listed in this guide are typically based on a standard double in high season, though we also list prices for suites and other types of rooms when applicable. Note, however, that precise rates can vary widely throughout the year, particularly at the chain hotels, where they can change almost daily depending on demand.

The Magic Kingdom

Contemporary Resort ☎407/824-1000.
The Disney monorail runs right through the center of this hotel, which takes its exterior design from the futuristic fantasies of the Magic Kingdom's Tomorrowland, but is disappointingly characterless inside. All the rooms have balconies, some affording good views of the Magic Kingdom fireworks. Rooms cost $244 and up.

Fort Wilderness Resort & Campground
☎407/824-2900. At this 700-acre site, you can pitch your tent, hook up your RV (from $35), or rent an air-conditioned six-berth cabin (from $229) – a good deal for larger groups. Entertainment includes nightly, open-air screenings of classic Disney movies, marshmallow roasts, and campfire sing-alongs.

Grand Floridian Resort & Spa
☎407/824-3000. Gabled roofs, verandas, and crystal chandeliers are among the frivolous variations on early Florida resort architecture at Disney's most upscale hotel. The elegant rooms provide a relaxing base from which to enjoy the sumptuous, full-service spa; and if you have money left over, you can rent a yacht to sail around the lake. Rooms from $349.

Polynesian Resort ☎407/824-2000.
Accessible via the monorail, this effective, if tacky, imitation of a Polynesian beach hotel is most enjoyable if you spend your time on the lakeside beach under the shade of coconut palms. The tropical theme is continued in the brightly colored rooms, which start at $304.

Wilderness Lodge ☎407/824-3200. This magnificent, oversized replica of a frontier log cabin is furnished with massive totem poles, a wood-burning fire in the lobby, and Southern-style wooden rocking chairs. The rooms, which are decorated in warm colors and follow a close-to-nature theme, start at $199.

EPCOT/Disney-MGM Studios

BoardWalk Resort ☎407/939-5100.
Styled after a 1930s mid-Atlantic seaside resort, complete with a waterfront promenade full of shops and restaurants, this resort goes to show that no theme is too humble for the Disney treatment. Starting at $294, the rooms have a spacious, if not overly warm, feel, and all come with balconies.

Caribbean Beach Resort ☎407/934-3400. Disney's first attempt at a budget-priced hotel has been quite a successful venture. The comfortable but unremarkable rooms (from $133) sprinkled about the nicely landscaped property are located in one of six "island villages," each with its own pool and beach.

Dolphin ☎407/934-4000. Topped by the giant sculpture of a dolphin and decorated in dizzying pastel shades and reproduction artwork from the likes of Matisse and Warhol, this hotel has rooms with a fresh, contemporary design costing $325 and up.

Pop Century Resort ☎407/938-4000.
With nearly 3000 rooms, this hotel devoted to mammoth pop icons from each decade of the second half of the twentieth century is Disney's largest. Like the *All-Star Resorts* (see opposite), the rooms are more basic than elsewhere in Disney and can be had for as little as $77.

Swan ☎407/934-3000. Separated by an artificial lake and beach from its sister hotel the *Dolphin*, the *Swan* is likewise whimsically decorated, though with sharper, more vibrant colors, and the rooms, starting at $325, are equipped with every conceivable luxury. Although both these hotels are on Disney property, they are not owned by Disney. For all practical purposes, however, this changes little; reservations can still be made through the Disney phone number or website.

Yacht and Beach Club Resorts
☎407/934-7000 (Yacht Club),
☎407/934-8000 (Beach Club). Turn-of-the-nineteenth-century New England is the cue for these twin hotels, complete with clapboard facades and a miniature lighthouse. Amusements include a small water

park reminiscent of a Nantucket beach. The bright and airy rooms are inspired by nautical themes and cost from $294 at both resorts.

Disney's Animal Kingdom

All-Star Resorts ☎ 407/939-6000 (Music), ☎ 407/939-5000 (Sports), ☎ 407/939-7000 (Movies). The most affordable of Disney's resorts, divided into the *All-Star Music Resort*, which is decorated with giant, brightly colored cowboy boots, guitar-shaped swimming pools, and the like; the *All-Star Sports Resort*, complete with huge Coca-Cola cups, American football helmets, and so on; and the *All-Star Movies Resort*, with humongous reminders of Disney movies looming over you. Each complex has its own pools and nearly 2000 rooms, which are on the simple side and as garishly decorated as the hotel exteriors, but start as low as $77.

Animal Kingdom Lodge ☎ 407/938-3000. One of Disney World's newest and most spectacular luxury accommodations, here you can wake up to see African wildlife grazing outside your window. The rooms are among the most attractive in Disney, done in warm colors and decorated with African handicrafts. You pay from $199 for a standard room or from $275 for a room with a view of the animal-filled savanna.

Coronado Springs Resort ☎ 407/939-1000. Named after explorer Don Francisco de Coronado, this moderately priced resort (rooms from $133 and up) pays homage to the cultures of Mexico and the American Southwest. The nearly 2000 rooms are built around a faux-Maya pyramid, while the informal but attractively styled food court is good for family meals, featuring Mexican food along with the usual burgers and pizzas.

Downtown Disney

Old Key West Resort ☎ 407/827-7700. Caribbean-style wooden villas and shaded verandas contribute to a tropical ambience based on a turn-of-the-nineteenth-century

Key West resort. Accommodation is in studios or villas, all equipped with kitchens. The studios sleep four and cost from $254; one-, two-, and three-bedroom villas are $340–1040.

Port Orleans Resort ☎ 407/934-5000. This resort combines two Southern themes: the row houses and cobbled streets of New Orleans at the *French Quarter*; and the grandiose manors overlooking the Mississippi River at the *Riverside*. Rooms are moderately priced at $133 and up, but have a somewhat spartan feel at the *Riverside*.

Saratoga Springs Resort & Spa ☎ 407/827-1100. Modeled on America's first vacation resort, Saratoga Springs, in the late 1800s, the accommodation is in spacious studios sleeping up to four (from $254) or well-equipped villas sleeping from four to twelve and including a whirlpool tub (from $340 to $1040). A third phase of the resort is scheduled to be finished in 2007, but noise from the construction site is not a major disturbance.

Lake Buena Vista

Embassy Suites 8100 Lake Ave ☎ 407/239-1144 or 1-800/EMBASSY, ⊛ www.embassysuitesorlando.com. Well-appointed two-room suites include refrigerators and microwaves and a free cooked-to-order breakfast. Excellent indoor and outdoor pools. Rates range from around $140 to $175.

Nickelodeon Family Suites by Holiday Inn 14500 Continental Gateway ☎ 407/387-5437 or 1-866/462-6425, ⊛ www.nickhotel.com. A true paradise for kids, with two giant swimming pools, each with elaborate water slides, free food if one accompanying adult pays for their meal, and even a spa for the little ones, plus a free shuttle to Disney and Universal. The accommodations are spacious and comfortable, with two-bedroom suites sleeping up to seven people starting at $225. Recommended.

Orlando World Center Marriott Resort 8701 World Center Drive ☎ 407/239-4200, ⊛ www.marriottworldcenter.com. Looking like a small city, this 2000-room hotel is the largest *Marriott* in the world. The

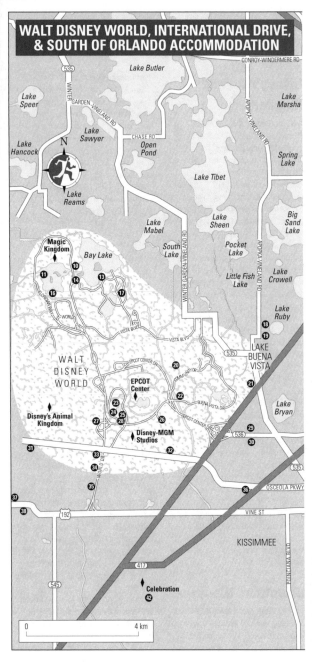

WALT DISNEY WORLD, INTERNATIONAL DRIVE, & SOUTH OF ORLANDO ACCOMMODATION

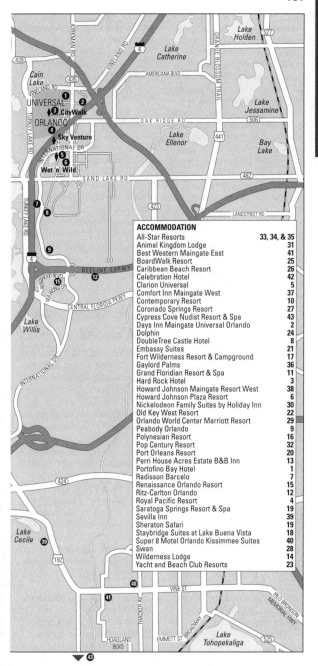

ACCOMMODATION

All-Star Resorts	33, 34, & 35
Animal Kingdom Lodge	31
Best Western Maingate East	41
BoardWalk Resort	25
Caribbean Beach Resort	26
Celebration Hotel	42
Clarion Universal	5
Comfort Inn Maingate West	37
Contemporary Resort	10
Coronado Springs Resort	27
Cypress Cove Nudist Resort & Spa	43
Days Inn Maingate Universal Orlando	2
Dolphin	24
DoubleTree Castle Hotel	8
Embassy Suites	21
Fort Wilderness Resort & Campground	17
Gaylord Palms	36
Grand Floridian Resort & Spa	11
Hard Rock Hotel	3
Howard Johnson Maingate Resort West	38
Howard Johnson Plaza Resort	6
Nickelodeon Family Suites by Holiday Inn	30
Old Key West Resort	22
Orlando World Center Marriott Resort	29
Peabody Orlando	9
Polynesian Resort	16
Pop Century Resort	32
Port Orleans Resort	20
Perri House Acres Estate B&B Inn	13
Portofino Bay Hotel	1
Radisson Barcelo	7
Renaissance Orlando Resort	15
Ritz-Carlton Orlando	12
Royal Pacific Resort	4
Saratoga Springs Resort & Spa	19
Sevilla Inn	39
Sheraton Safari	
Staybridge Suites at Lake Buena Vista	18
Super 8 Motel Orlando Kissimmee Suites	40
Swan	28
Wilderness Lodge	14
Yacht and Beach Club Resorts	23

rooms are comfortable without being overly luxurious, while the giant lagoon-shaped swimming pool with water slide, the four tennis courts, and the well-manicured golf course that snakes around the resort make this an excellent place for recreational activities. The high-season room rate is $369.

Perri House Acres Estate B&B Inn 10417 Vista Oaks Court ☎407/876-4830 or 1-800/780-4830, ⊛www.perrihouse .com. This friendly eight-room bed and breakfast hidden on four wooded acres – which is also a bird sanctuary – lies just a stone's throw from the opulent resorts of Disney and is the perfect antidote to all the theme-park frenzy. The clean and bright rooms have their own private outside entrances and cost from $99. You'll also find a swimming pool and hot tub.

Sheraton Safari 12205 S Apopka-Vineland Rd ☎407/239-0444 or 1-800/423-3297, ⊛www.sheratonsafari.com. Based on an African-safari theme (including a water slide in the form of a giant python), this is one of a cluster of hotels less than half a mile from the entrance to Downtown Disney. The rooms are tastefully decorated, free of leopard-skin rugs, and start at around $109.

Staybridge Suites at Lake Buena Vista 8751 Suiteside Drive ☎407/238-0777. Next to the *Sheraton Safari*, but slightly removed from the other hotels in the vicinity, this place benefits from a more soothing atmosphere as a result. The spacious one- and two-bedroom suites (from $139 and $159 respectively) have particularly well-equipped kitchens, DVD players, and sometimes even two bathrooms. A buffet breakfast is included.

Universal Orlando

Hard Rock Hotel. Stuffed with rock 'n' roll memorabilia, and with familiar tunes blaring out at poolside, this is the least tranquil of the park's resorts – and the most popular with the younger generation. The simple yet stylish rooms (from $254) are equipped with high-quality CD players.

Portofino Bay Hotel. This lavish re-creation of the Italian seaside village of Portofino has vintage Alfa Romeos and Fiats parked

in the piazza, as well as authentic Italian furniture and marble accents in the luxurious rooms, which cost $329 and up. Enjoy every possible luxury, including a full-service spa, at one of the top-rated hotels in Florida.

Royal Pacific Resort. While there's nothing that original about the South Pacific island theme, the kids will enjoy the lagoon-style pool, and the rooms, decked in bamboo and other tropical accents, are very comfortable. It's also the most economical of Universal's resorts, with rooms starting at $229.

International Drive and around

Clarion Universal 7299 Universal Blvd ☎407/351-5009 or 1-800/445-7299, ⊛www.clarionuniversal.com. This mid-sized, easy-going hotel has nicely furnished rooms that sleep up to four, which, at around $70, are good value. It's also in a prime location for visits to Universal Orlando and Wet 'n' Wild.

Days Inn Maingate Universal Orlando 5827 Caravan Court ☎407/351-3800 or 1-800/777-3297, ⊛www.orlandoflus .com. Within walking distance of Universal Orlando and also close to the action on International Drive, the rooms at this branch of the nationwide chain are nothing fancy, but do sleep up to four and are reasonably priced at around $70, especially given the hotel's proximity to Universal. Kids under 12 eat free if accompanied by a paying adult.

DoubleTree Castle Hotel 8629 International Drive ☎407/345-1511 or 1-800/952-2785, ⊛www.doubletree castle.com. This elaborate theme hotel, complete with Renaissance music and medieval decor, such as suits of armor, offers comfortable rooms from around $120, plus free transportation to the theme parks – and complimentary chocolate-chip cookies.

Howard Johnson Plaza Resort 7050 S Kirkman Rd ☎407/351-2000 or 1-800/327-3808, ⊛ www.howardjohnson hotelorlando.com. Decently sized rooms, three pools, and free shuttle buses to the major theme parks make this a good base for nondrivers concentrating on the big attractions. The very reasonable rates start at around $50.

Peabody Orlando 9801 International Drive ☎407/352-4000 or 1-800/PEA-BODY, ⊛ www.peabodyorlando.com. The twenty-seven stories of opulent rooms are primarily aimed at delegates using the massive Orange County Convention Center across the street. If money is no object and you like lots of in-room luxuries, access to a fitness center, and floodlit tennis courts, this one's for you. Ducks parade through the lobby twice a day. Rooms can cost anything from around $150 in low season to $400 in high season.

Radisson Barcelo 8444 International Drive ☎407/345-0505 or 1-888/380-9696, ⊛ www.radisson-orlando.com. Those looking for relaxation and convenience will find the spacious rooms (sleeping up to four; from $75) and the excellent location, directly opposite The Mercado in the heart of I-Drive, a winning combination. Speed-swimming records have been set at the adjacent YMCA's Olympic-sized pool, to which hotel guests have free access.

Renaissance Orlando Resort 6677 Sea Harbor Drive ☎407/351-5555 or 1-800/327-6677. This upscale hotel is perfectly situated for visiting SeaWorld Orlando and also in a prime location for easy access to I-Drive, Universal, and Disney. The very spacious and comfortable rooms (usually around $170–210) are built around a bright and airy atrium in which one of Orlando's finest Champagne brunches is served every Sunday ($34.95).

Ritz-Carlton Orlando 4012 Central Florida Parkway ☎407/206-2400, ⊛ www .grandelakes.com. Definitely one of Orlando's most luxurious hotels, this elegant building with an intimate feel and superb

rooms shares the 500-acre Grande Lakes Orlando – the hotel's landscaped grounds – with another excellent hotel, the *JW Marriott*, and a spacious golf course. The spa uses lots of citrus in its treatments, while the fitness center (free for guests) offers a tremendous range of state-of-the-art equipment. Rooms start at $249.

Downtown Orlando

See map on p.124.

The Courtyard at Lake Lucerne 211 N Lucerne Circle E ☎407/648-5188, ⊛ www.orlandohistoricinn.com. A lush flower garden and four separate antique inns, one of which is the oldest house in Orlando, comprise this peaceful oasis of grace and hospitality nestled right in the busy downtown area. The very eclectic choice of accommodations range from elegantly furnished Victorian- and Edwardian-era rooms ($115–225) to airy Art Deco suites ($89–120).

Embassy Suites 191 E Pine St ☎407/841-1000, ⊛ www.embassyorlandodowntown .com. All 167 suites ($149–209) of this stylish high-rise open onto a busy atrium, although noise is not a problem. Each suite has two rooms, a microwave, and a fridge. A cooked-to-order breakfast and evening cocktail reception are included in the price.

Eō Inn 227 N Eola Drive ☎407/481-8485 or 1-888/481-8488, ⊛ www.eoinn.com. Right on Lake Eola, this chic boutique hotel has understated but stylish rooms ($129) with modern furnishings and sometimes lake views ($219). The spa offers a full range of massages, facials, and other such treatments, and there's an inviting hot-tub on the rooftop terrace.

Parliament House Resort 410 N Orange Blossom Trail, just east of downtown ☎407/425-7571, ⊛ www.parliament house.com. This well-known gay resort has been given a shot in the arm by a recent change of management, resulting in much more efficient service. You'll find several bars, a disco, a pool, a lakeside beach, drag shows, plenty of activities, and 130 simple, yet comfortable, renovated rooms in the $60–100 range.

Travelodge 409 N Magnolia Ave ☏ 407/423-1671, ⊛ www.travelodge .com. This motel-style accommodation is within walking distance of everything. Due to the central location and low prices, it fills up very quickly on the weekends, so reserve in advance for Friday and Saturday nights. There's also a small pool and free local calls. From $55.

Veranda Bed & Breakfast Inn 115 N Summerlin Ave ☏ 407/849-0321 or 1-800/420-6822, ⊛ www.theveranda bandb.com. Housed in five period buildings that sit around a courtyard garden and swimming pool, this pretty, but slightly precious, twelve-room bed and breakfast enjoys a good location in the trendy Thornton Park district, one block from Lake Eola. Singles start from $99, doubles from $109.

Westin Grand Bohemian 325 S Orange Ave ☏ 407/313-9000 or 1-866/663-0024, ⊛ www.grandbohemianhotel .com. Downtown's most luxurious hotel occupies an imposing building across from City Hall, full of works of art and lovely rooms decorated in soothing, earthy tones. Guests have access to a heated outdoor pool and a fitness center. High-season rates are $369, but fall to $209 at quieter times.

Winter Park

See map on pp.132–133.

Best Western Mount Vernon Inn 110 S Orlando Ave, a twenty-minute walk west of Park Avenue ☏ 407/647-1166 or 1-800/992-3379. A perfectly satisfactory mid-range hotel with tastefully decorated rooms for $114, a pool, and a small bar.

Park Plaza 307 S Park Ave ☏ 407/647-1072 or 1-800/228-7220, ⊛ www .parkplazahotel.com. Reminiscent of New Orleans' French Quarter, this 1920s hotel is stuffed with wonderful wicker furniture and brass fittings. Rooms start at $117 and some have balconies overlooking either Park Avenue or Central Park. Be sure to book early. A continental breakfast is included.

South of Orlando

Best Western Maingate East 4018 W Vine St ☏ 407/870-2000, ⊛ www .bestwesternhotel-orlando.com. Forced to close after the spate of hurricanes that hit Florida in 2004, this quiet property now offers comfy renovated rooms (from $89) and a pool area affording good views of the small planes landing at the nearby municipal airport. Free shuttle to Disney.

Celebration Hotel 700 Bloom St ☏ 407/566-6000 or 1-888/499-3800, ⊛ www.celebrationhotel.com. Celebration's only hotel is as upscale and picturesque as the town itself – and one of the most peaceful places to stay in the Orlando area. Most of the compact but elegant rooms overlook the lake, as does the attractive deck that skirts one side of the hotel and contains a small swimming pool and an intimate hot-tub. From $249.

Comfort Inn Maingate West 9330 W Irlo Bronson Memorial Hwy, five minutes west of Disney ☏ 407/424-8420 or 1-800/440-4473. The yellow exterior of this pleasant hotel is a foretaste of the bright, cheerful, and slightly garish rooms inside. Continental breakfast and local calls are included. Rates from $50.

Cypress Cove Nudist Resort & Spa 4425 Pleasant Hill Rd, Kissimmee ☏ 407/933-5870 or 1-888/683-3140, ⊛ www .cypresscoveresort.com. This full-service resort caters to those who like to vacation in the nude. You'll find a range of activities and amenities, including tennis courts, fitness center, swimming pool, restaurants, plus a choice of spacious apartments, hotel rooms, or camping. Weekday rates are $72 for a hotel room or $14.50 for an RV hook-up, plus a daily membership fee of $20–30.

Gaylord Palms 6000 W Osceola Parkway ☏ 407/586-0000, ⊛ www.gaylordpalms .com. Dominated by its huge atrium based on an Everglades theme, complete with live alligators, turtles, and snakes, this upscale hotel has stylish rooms (particularly in the *Emerald Bay* section), all with their own computers providing free Internet access. You can relax at the luxurious spa and two swimming pools, and work out in the well-equipped fitness center. Rooms start at $239.

Howard Johnson Maingate Resort West 8660 W Irlo Bronson Memorial Hwy ☎407/396-4500 or 1-800/638-7829, ⓦwww.orlandohojomaingate.com. An elaborate *HoJo* with no less than three pools, two restaurants, tennis, volleyball, shuffleboard, and fitness center, as well as free transportation to the Disney parks. The recently renovated rooms with new beds, furniture, and carpets cost $50–80.

Sevilla Inn 4640 W Irlo Bronson Memorial Hwy ☎407/396-4135 or 1-800/367-1363, ⓦwww.sevillainn.com. A refreshing change from the chain hotels, this unpretentious privately owned motel has simple, cheap ($45), and perfectly satisfactory rooms and a humble pool.

Super 8 Motel Orlando Kissimmee Suites 1815 W Vine St ☎407/847-6121 or 1-800/325-4348, ⓦwww.abcsuites .com. Choose from standard rooms ($40; sleep up to four) or apartment-style suites ($70; sleep up to 6) in an attractive garden setting; the latter come complete with full kitchen, living and dining areas, and two bedrooms. Free continental breakfast.

Essentials

Arrival

Most people arrive in Orlando via the international airport, from where you'll find numerous public transport and taxi options for getting to anywhere in Orlando. The train and bus stations, meanwhile, are both close to downtown Orlando.

By air

Orlando International Airport (T 407/825-2001, W www.orlandoairports .net) lies nine miles southeast of downtown Orlando. The local **Lynx buses** (see p.170) link the airport with downtown and International Drive. For downtown, use #11 or #51 (both take around 45 minutes); for International Drive, use #42 (around 60 minutes). All buses depart from Level 1 of the airport's Main Terminal (on the "A Side" concourse) every 30 minutes between 5.30am and 11.30pm for #11, 5.30am and 10.30pm for #51, and 6am to 10.30pm for #42.

More expensive **shuttle buses**, such as those operated by Mears Transportation (T 407/423-5566, W www .mearstransportation.com), will carry you from the airport to any hotel or motel in the Orlando area. The flat rate from the airport to a hotel on International Drive or downtown Orlando is $15; to Walt Disney World, Lake Buena Vista, or US-192 the fare is $17.

A **taxi** (see p.171) to downtown Orlando, International Drive, or the motels on US-192 will cost anywhere from $30 to $60; Walt Disney World is $50 to $60.

All of the main **car rental** companies (see p.175) either have offices in the airport terminal itself or a short free shuttle bus-ride away.

A second airport, **Orlando/Sanford International** (T 407/585-4000, W www.orlandosanfordairport.com), is a small but growing facility twenty miles north of downtown Orlando that receives a lot of charter flights from the UK. A taxi from Sanford to downtown Orlando costs around $55; or you could save money by taking a taxi to the Seminole Center, a shopping center on the corner of US-17/92 and Lake Mary, and then catching Lynx #39 into downtown Orlando (every 30 minutes from 4.30am to 10.30pm; journey time 70 minutes).

By bus and train

Long-distance **buses** arrive at the Orlando **Greyhound** terminal, 555 N John Young Parkway (T 407/292-3422), from where you can catch Lynx #25 into downtown (every 30 minutes from 5.30am to 1.20am; journey time 10 minutes). If you're staying along US-192, consider going to the Kissimmee Greyhound terminal, 103 E Dakin St (T 407/847-3911), which is considerably closer.

Arriving by **train**, you'll wind up at the Orlando **Amtrak** station, 1400 Slight Blvd (T 407/843-7611). To get to downtown from here, take Lynx #50 (every hour from 5.50am to 12.50am; journey time 10 minutes). Again, if you're staying along US-192, the station in Kissimmee, 111 E Dakin Ave (T 407/933-1170), is much more convenient. There is another station in Winter Park, 150 W Morse Blvd (T 407/645-5055).

By car

For **drivers**, the major cross-Florida roads intersect in or around Orlando. The **I-4** passes southwest–northeast through Walt Disney World and downtown Orlando and is the road you should take for Tampa and the nearest coastal beaches; **US-192** (the Irlo Bronson Memorial Highway) crosses I-4 just south of Disney and charts an east–west course fifteen miles south of Orlando. **Hwy-528** (the Beeline Expressway) stems from International Drive and heads for the east coast. And **Florida's Turnpike** (for which there is a toll) cuts northwest–southeast, avoiding Disney and downtown Orlando altogether, but continuing to major destinations in south Florida.

Information

Despite the "Tourist Information Center" signs outside virtually every gift shop and the mass of brochures and magazines available nearly everywhere you look, the best source of reliable information is the **Official Visitor Center**, 8723 International Drive (daily 8am–7pm; ☎ 407/363-5872, ⊛ www.orlandoinfo.com), where you should pick up the free *Orlando Official Visitors Guide* and browse through the hundreds of leaflets and coupons; discounted attraction tickets are also sold here (daily 8am–6pm). You can call a Visitor Center Travel Counselor (☎ 1-800/972-3304), who will book vacation packages and offer useful vacation planning tips.

The **Winter Park Chamber of Commerce**, 150 New York Ave (Mon–Fri 9am–5pm; ☎ 407/644-8281, ⊛ www.winterpark.org), has good local information and brochures not found at the Official Visitor Center. If you're using the motels along US-192, drop by the equally well-stocked **Kissimmee–St Cloud Convention & Visitors Bureau**, 1925 E Irlo Bronson Memorial Hwy in Kissimmee (Mon–Fri 8am–5pm; ☎ 407/847-5000 or 1-800/333-KISS, ⊛ www.floridakiss.com). The best entertainment guide to the area is the Friday "Calendar" section of the *Orlando Sentinel* newspaper.

In addition to the tourist-office websites, you'll find a wealth of Orlando information on the Web. ⊛ **www.orlandocitybeat.com** is a user-friendly site with a comprehensive listing of cultural events, social gatherings, and nighttime activities; ⊛ **www.allearsnet.com** is one of the best "unofficial" guides to Walt Disney World, not least for its regularly updated listings of menus at every restaurant on Disney property; and ⊛ **www.theotherorlando.com** contains some equally good information on Orlando's other main attractions, including Universal and SeaWorld.

Getting around

Orlando is a sprawling city and, although you can get around on public transportation, it is either very time consuming or expensive depending on the mode you choose. The only place where public transportation is easy, quick (and free) is at Walt Disney World, where buses, boats, and a monorail provide regular links between the attractions and the resorts. Drivers should note that rush-hour traffic in Orlando is severe, so allow extra time if you are driving in the late afternoon and early evening.

Buses

Local **Lynx** buses (☎ 407/841-LYNX, ⊛ www.golynx.com) converge at the downtown **Lynx Central Station**, 455 N Garland Ave. Most routes operate from 6.30am to 8pm on weekdays, 7.30am to 6pm on Saturdays, and 8am to 6pm on Sundays (although sometimes routes don't operate at all on Sundays). You'll need **exact change** ($1.50 one-way; $3.50 day-pass) if you pay on board; a weekly pass costs $12 at the central station. The single fare includes a free transfer to another Lynx service, valid for travel within 90 minutes of the initial ticket purchase. Given the expanse of the network and the considerable journey times, you'll often be hard-pressed to catch your second bus before the ticket expires. The Lynx system makes around 4000 stops in three counties, and the Official Visitors Center (see above) has a very useful handout entitled *How to Get Where on the Lynx Bus System*, which explains how to get to many points of interest by bus starting from International Drive.

The **I-Ride Trolley** (☎407/248-9590 or 1-866/243-7483, ⓦ www.iridetrolley .com) serves all points along International Drive (including SeaWorld Orlando), running between the Belz Factory Outlet World shopping mall in the north and Orlando Premium Outlets in the south. It operates roughly every twenty minutes daily from 8am to 10.30pm, costing 75¢ one-way (seniors 25¢); exact change is required, and children 12 and under ride free. One-day passes for unlimited travel are also available for $3.

Taxis and shuttle buses

Orlando **taxis** are expensive: rates begin at $3.25 for the first mile, plus $1.75 for each additional mile. For non-drivers, however, they're the only way to get around at night – try Town & Country (☎407/828-3035), Star Taxi (☎407/857-9999), or Yellow Cab (☎407/699-9999).

Cheaper than taxis, but more expensive and quicker than local buses, are the **shuttle buses**, minivans, or coaches run by private companies connecting the main accommodation areas, such as International Drive and US-192, with Walt Disney World, SeaWorld Orlando, and Universal Orlando. You should phone at least a day ahead to be picked up, and confirm a time for your return. Mears Transportation Group (☎407/423-5566, ⓦ www .mearstransportation.com) charges $12–14 for a round-trip ride from International Drive or US-192 to all the major attractions.

Driving

The single most useful route for getting around Orlando by car is the **I-4**, which dissects the city in a southwest–northeast direction and has exits for Walt Disney World, SeaWorld Orlando, International Drive, Universal Orlando, and downtown Orlando. I-4 also intersects with **US-192** (exit 64AB), the busy east–west corridor south of Orlando, which, unlike I-4, is not an Interstate and so has intermittent traffic lights.

There is an $8 **parking** fee at Walt Disney World, Universal Orlando (free for Disney and Universal resort guests), and SeaWorld Orlando, but not Discovery Cove. At the more upscale hotels you often have to pay an additional fee to use their parking facilities. In downtown Orlando, metered parking is in effect during the day; after 6pm and on the weekends parking is free. Finding a space, however, is another matter, particularly on Friday and Saturday nights, and city garages and several privately owned parking lots (charging a flat rate of typically $5) cater to the overflow.

Cycling

Cycling isn't a practical option for getting around Orlando because the distances are simply too long and few of the roads are suitable (or safe) for cyclists. However, if you'd like to explore the countryside on two wheels, the nearest **bike trail** is the nineteen-mile West Orange Trail, starting just west of Orlando at the County Line Station (take Hwy-50 towards Clermont) and ending in the town of Apopka. **Rent bikes** at West Orange Trail Bikes & Blades, located along the trail at 17914 Hwy-438, Winter Garden (☎ 407/877-0600 or 1-888/281-3341).

Theme park practicalities

The opening hours, ticket prices, and other practicalities of visiting Orlando's main theme parks are explained below.

Walt Disney World

☎ 407/824-4321, ⊛ www.disneyworld .com. Opening times vary greatly depending on the park you are visiting and the time of the year. The parks are generally **open** daily from 9am to around 9pm or 10pm during holidays and in the summer, and from 9am to 6pm or later the rest of the year, with extended hours on holidays. Disney's Animal Kingdom closes at 5pm. During peak seasons the *Orlando Sentinel* lists each park's hours on the front page. Every day, one of the four main parks either opens one hour earlier or closes three hours later for **guests of the Disney resorts** only.

The basic single-day, one-park **admission price** is the same for all Disney parks: $59.75 for adults and $48 for children aged 3 to 9. The **Magic Your Way** option allows you to choose the number of days you wish to spend visiting the parks and pay a significantly reduced price compared with the single-day admission – for example, a seven-day ticket would cost $199 (adult) or $160 (children 3–11). Magic Your Way tickets can be bought for a maximum of ten days and you can only visit one park per day. If you want the freedom to move from park to park in the same day, you must add the **Park Hopper** option for an additional flat fee of $35 on top of the basic Magic Your Way ticket. The **Magic Plus Pack** option allows you to add from two to five extra admissions (the exact number depends on the length of your basic Magic Your Way ticket) to Blizzard Beach, Typhoon Lagoon, DisneyQuest, Disney's Wide World of Sports, and Pleasure Island for a flat fee of $45.

In an effort to reduce waiting times, Disney has established the **FASTPASS** system. At certain attractions you can obtain a FASTPASS by inserting your park ticket into a special FASTPASS ticket station. The machine gives you a slip indicating the time you should return to the attraction. In effect you book a time to enter the FASTPASS line, which bypasses the regular line and gets you into the attraction with little or no wait. Note that you can only hold one FASTPASS for one attraction at any one time. Special tips on **saving time** and beating the crowds are detailed under the individual park accounts. The single most effective way of avoiding the crowds, however, is to visit during the quietest periods, generally January, May, and September. The busiest

Disney Line cruises

Disney has been in the cruise ship business since 1998. Its two elegant ships, *Disney Magic* and *Disney Wonder*, depart from Port Canaveral, an hour from the theme parks. The ships are designed with the family in mind, but offer touches of luxury – including inlaid Italian woodwork – that will impress regular cruise-goers. The on-board entertainment caters to children and adults alike. You'll find the type of live shows that abound at the theme parks, delighting the little ones with appearances by plenty of Disney characters, but also comedy evenings, piano bars, and nightclubs for adults. Likewise, there is a variety of food and restaurants for young and old, ranging from French and Italian cuisine served in elegant dining rooms to buffets and snack bars to satiate less discriminating appetites. The cruises themselves last three, four, or seven days. The three- and four-day options sail to Nassau and then to Disney's own Bahamian island, Castaway Cay. You can either combine the seven-day cruise with three or four days at sea and three or four days at a Disney resort or spend the whole seven days at sea, touring either the Eastern or Western Caribbean. Prices vary considerably depending on when you go and the cabin (or Disney resort) that you choose. Three-day cruises range from $399 to $2849 per person (excluding airfare); four-day cruises are $499 to $3249; and the different types of seven-day cruises are $799 to $5199. Parking is $30, $40, and $70 for the three-, four-, and seven-day cruises respectively.

For more information, call ☎1-800/951-3532 or log on to ⊛www.disneycruise line.com.

times are summertime, around Thanksgiving (the fourth Thursday in November), Christmas, and Easter.

Universal Orlando

Half a mile north of I-4 exits 74B or 75A ☎407/363-8000, ⊛www.uescape.com. Both Universal Studios and Islands of Adventure **open** at 9am and close at any time between 6pm and 10pm depending on the season.

The basic single-day, one-park **admission price** is $59.75 for adults and $48 for children aged 3 to 9 – exactly the same as Disney. Universal also offers various ways to reduce the cost of admission provided you are prepared to spread your visit over a number of days. A **2-Day/2-Park Ticket** costs $104.95 (adults) and $94.95 (children 3–9), while the **Orlando FlexTicket** offers unlimited admission for fourteen days to both of the Universal parks – as well as SeaWorld Orlando and Wet 'n' Wild – for $184.95 (adults) and $150.95 (children 3–9).

Universal's equivalent to Disney's FASTPASS is called **Universal Express** and it works in virtually the same way. To avoid the limitation of being able to hold only one Universal Express pass for one attraction at any one time you can pay $25 (cheaper rates apply at quieter times of the year) for **Universal Express Plus**, which allows you to enter the Universal Express line whenever and wherever you like. **Guests of the Universal resorts** can also join the Universal Express lines simply by presenting their room key-card.

SeaWorld Orlando

Sea Harbor Drive, at the intersection of I-4 and the Beeline Expressway ☎ 407/351-3600 or 1-800/327-2424, ⊛www.seaworld.com. The park **opens** at 9am and closes at any time between 6pm and 11pm depending on the season.

The basic single-day **admission price** is $59.75 for adults and $48 for children aged 3 to 9 – once again, identical to Disney and Universal. However, for only a few dollars more you can buy a **Fun Card**, which, for $64.95 (adults) and $54.95 (children 3–9), entitles you to unlimited entry to SeaWorld for the whole of the year of your visit. The **Orlando Flex Ticket** also includes SeaWorld.

Discovery Cove

Next to SeaWorld Orlando on Central Florida Parkway ☎ 407/370-1280 or 1-877/4-DISCOVERY, ◉ www.discovery cove.com. The park is **open** from 9am to 5.30pm throughout the year. The **admission price** for adults and children if you include the dolphin swim is $229 from January to mid-March, $259 from mid-March to October, and $239 from November to December. You can opt to not take the dolphin swim, in which case the price is $129 from January to mid-March, $159 from mid-March to October, and $139 from November to December. Since the number of guests is limited to no more than 1000 per day, you must make a reservation to visit Discovery Cove. For visits including the dolphin swim, reserve one to three months in advance; otherwise, reserve at least three weeks ahead of time. All tickets include admission to either SeaWorld Orlando or Busch Gardens for seven consecutive days.

Busch Gardens

300 E Busch Blvd, Tampa, two miles east of I-275 or two miles west of I-75 ☎ 1-888/800-5447, ◉ www.buschgardens .com. The park generally **opens** at 9am or 9.30am and closes at 6pm or 7pm, except for July when it closes at 10pm.

The basic single-day **admission price** is $55.95 for adults and $45.95 for children aged 3 to 9. As at SeaWorld Orlando, buying a **Fun Card** represents much better value for money. For $61.95 (adults) and $51.95 (children 3–9), you can get unlimited entry to Busch Gardens for the whole of the year of your visit. The **Orlando FlexTicket** can be extended to cover Busch Gardens for $224.95 (adults), and $189.95 (children 3–9). This includes a free shuttle bus to the park from Orlando (for departure times and pick-up points, call ☎ 1-800/221-1339).

Festivals and events

Late January
Zora Neale Hurston Festival of the Arts and Humanities ☎ 407/647-3307, ◉ www.zorafestival.com. Taking over the historic town of Eatonville for five days, this festival celebrates African-American culture. You can buy a ticket at the gate to enter the festival grounds, where you'll witness music, dance, and theatrical performances.

Mid-February
Daytona 500 ☎ 386/253-7223, ◉ www .daytonainternationalspeedway.com. Attended by none other than George W. Bush in 2005, this is the most prestigious stock-car race in NASCAR's Nextel Cup Series. Tickets are expensive ($95 and up) and should be bought well in advance from the Daytona International Speedway.

Late February/early March
Bach Festival ☎ 407/646-2182, ◉ www .bachfestivalflorida.org. Top musicians, orchestras, and choirs converge on Rollins College in Winter Park to pay homage to the works of Bach and other composers.

Early March
Daytona Bike Week ◉ www.officialbike week.com. Motorcycle races, rallies and parades, plenty of posing, and a spot of raucous behavior thrown in for good measure epitomize this famous annual gathering of thousands of bikers in the seaside town of Daytona Beach.

Late March/early April
Florida Film Festival ☎ 407/644-6579, ◉ www.enzian.org. A well-respected event on the US film festival circuit, showcasing documentaries, narrative and short films, animation, and films from Florida, many of them screened at the Enzian Theater in Maitland.

Mid-April to early June
EPCOT International Flower and Garden Festival ☎ 407/934-7639. Each weekend

of the festival features lectures on gardening, bugs, and even making perfume, along with more light-hearted entertainment, all against the backdrop of EPCOT's stunning flower displays made from 30 million blooms.

Early June

Gay Day ⊛www.gayday.com. Over 100,000 gays and lesbians descend on Walt Disney World and Universal Orlando, visiting the parks by day and filling Downtown Disney's clubs at night. The event actually lasts four days.

Late May

Orlando International Fringe Festival ☎407/648-0077, ⊛www .orlandofringe.org. A ten-day event where over 300 performers perform 500 shows, from drama and musicals to comedy and mime.

July 4

All of the main theme parks put on some kind of special display involving plenty of flag-waving, patriotic music, and fireworks for American Independence Day. There are also games, entertainment, and yet more fireworks around Lake Eola in downtown Orlando.

Mid-October

Silver Spurs Rodeo ☎321/697-3495, ⊛www.silverspursrodeo.com. The largest rodeo east of the Mississippi gets going in the Silver Spurs Arena in Kissimmee, where cowboys come from all over to compete during four days for prize-money in the thousands of dollars.

Late October

FUNAI Classic ☎407/835-42525. Towards the end of the professional golf season the PGA Tour stages a competition at Disney's Magnolia and Palm golf courses.

Directory

AIRLINES

Aer Lingus ☎1-800/IRISH-AIR, ⊛www .aerlingus.com; **Air Canada** ☎1-888/247-2262, ⊛www.aircanada.com; **Air Transat** ☎1-800/587-2672, ⊛www .airtransat.com; **Alaska Airlines** ☎1-800/252-7522, ⊛www.alaska-air.com; **Alitalia** ☎1-800/223-5730, ⊛www .alitalia.com; **America West Airlines** ☎1-800/235-9292, ⊛www.americawest.com; **American Airlines** ☎1-800/433-7300, ⊛www.aa.com; **Austrian Airlines** ☎1-800/843-0002, ⊛www.aua.com; **British Airways** ☎1-800/AIRWAYS, ⊛www .ba.com; **Continental Airlines domestic** ☎1-800/523-FARE, international ☎1-800/231-0856, ⊛www.continental.com; **Delta domestic** ☎1-800/221-1212, international ☎1-800/241-4141, ⊛www .delta.com; **Iberia** ☎1-800/772-4642, ⊛www.iberia.com; **Northwest domestic** ☎1-800/225-2525, international ☎1-800/447-4747, ⊛www.nwa.com; **United Airlines domestic** ☎1-800/241-6522, international ☎1-800/538-2929, ⊛www .united.com; **US Airways domestic** ☎1-800/428-4322, international ☎1-800/622-1015, ⊛www.usair.com; **Virgin Atlantic** ☎1-800/862-8621, ⊛www .virgin-atlantic.com.

BANKS AND MONEY

Banks are generally open Mon–Thurs 10am–3pm, Fri 10am–5pm. Credit and debit cards are accepted everywhere. You can either use them to pay for things directly or withdraw money from ATM machines (note that ATM withdrawals using credit cards are treated as cash advances, with interest accruing daily). US-dollar travelers' checks can be used in shops, restaurants, and the like, or cashed in banks. Travelers' checks in other currencies are more difficult to change.

CAR RENTAL

All the main car-rental firms have offices at or close to Orlando International Airport. Demand is strong despite the high rates (around $30 per day or $225 per week for a mid-sized car), so call in advance during busy seasons.

Avis ☎1-800/831-2847, ⊛www.avis.com; **Alamo** ☎1-800/327-9633, ⊛www.alamo .com; **Budget** ☎1-800/527-0700, ⊛www .budgetrentacar.com; **Dollar** ☎1-800/800-4000, ⊛www.dollar.com; **National** ☎1-800/227-7368, ⊛www.nationalcar.com.

CINEMAS

Orlando's cinemas tend to be in out-of-the-way shopping malls. The most easily accessible multi-screen complexes, which show the latest Hollywood releases, are in Downtown Disney, CityWalk, and Pointe Orlando on International Drive. If you're staying along US-192, there is a 21-screen Muivico Cinema at the Osceola Square Mall, 3831 W Vine St, while downtown Orlando has the Downtown Media Arts Center, 39 S Magnolia Ave, a small cinema screening independent and art-house films. Many of the films shown during the Florida Film Festival (see p.174) are at the Enzian Theater, 1300 S Orlando Ave, Maitland.

CONSULATES
French American Institute of Orlando, 522 E Washington St ☎407/839-0581; **Netherlands** 400 S Orange Ave ☎407/425-8000; **UK** 200 S Orange Ave ☎407/426-7855.

DISABLED TRAVELERS
Orlando is very well equipped for disabled visitors. The major theme parks are all wheelchair-friendly, as are city buses. Many hotels have rooms specifically designed to meet the needs of the disabled and most public buildings have at least one toilet for the disabled. Many attractions and services also have a special phone line dedicated to the hearing impaired.

DENTISTS
Dentist referral ☎407/894-9798.

DOCTORS
Doc at your Door (house calls) ☎407/970-3138.

ELECTRICITY
110V AC.

EMERGENCIES
For police, fire, or ambulance services, call ☎911.

GAY AND LESBIAN VISITORS
Orlando's gay scene is nowhere near as vibrant as it is farther south in places such as Key West and Fort Lauderdale. There is, however, a handful of bars and clubs for gays and lesbians as well as sporadic social events. Gay Day (see p.175) in early June draws hundreds of thousands of gays and lesbians to the area. Keep abreast of what's going on at ☎www.gayorlando.com.

GOLF
There are over 125 golf courses in the Greater Orlando area. Green fees can vary from around $50 to well over $100 for eighteen holes depending on when and where you play. The rates normally include the rental of an electric cart. Walt Disney World alone has five eighteen-hole golf courses, including the Magnolia and Palm courses which host the PGA Tour's FUNAI Classic in October. To book tee times at a Disney course, call ☎407/939-4653. Some of the Orlando area's other highly regarded

courses include: Celebration Golf Club, 701 Golf Park Drive, Celebration (☎407/566-4653, ☎www.celebrationgolf; green fees $78–119), Falcon's Fire, 3200 Seralago Blvd, Kissimmee (☎407/239-5445, ☎www .falconsfire.com; green fees $77–118), and the *El Campeono* course at Mission Inn, 10400 County Rd 48, Howey-in-the-Hills – 35 minutes northwest of Orlando (☎1-800/874-9053, ☎www.missioninnresort .com; green fees $60–85). For further descriptions and rates of Orlando courses, see ☎www.playfloridagolf.com.

INTERNET
Many hotels have one or two computers with Internet access – either in fancy "business centers" at the more upscale establishments, for which there is a charge of around $10 per hour, or free at the budget hotels. If you have your own laptop computer, you can connect to the Internet in most hotel rooms via the telephone line. In some rooms an Ethernet cable is provided for high-speed access, which is sometimes free but normally costs around $10 per day. There are WiFi Hotspots in some cafés, shopping malls, and other public places.

PHOTOGRAPHY
Photography is encouraged at the theme parks, especially with the costumed characters that mingle with guests (there is no extra charge if you take the picture with your own camera). Photography is not allowed on the rollercoasters, although strategically placed cameras take digital shots of riders in various stages of terror and can be ordered (usually for around $10) upon leaving the ride. The use of a flash is also prohibited on most rides and during the live shows involving humans and animals.

POST OFFICES
Post offices are generally open Monday to Friday 9am–5pm and Saturday 9am–noon. The actual branches, however, are often stuck out in shopping malls and other obscure locations, so posting letters and postcards is more practically done using the blue mail boxes found on street corners or through your hotel concierge. One location relatively close to the resorts is at the Shoppes at Buena Vista ☎407/238-0223 (Mon–Fri 9am–4pm, Sat 9am to noon).

SPAS
Some of the more upscale resorts such as the *Ritz-Carlton Orlando*, *Gaylord Palms*, and Disney's *Grand Floridian Resort & Spa* have on-site spas offering the full range of massages and other treatments to guests and non-guests alike.

TAX

A 6.5 percent sales tax is added to virtually everything you buy in a shop, as well as to things such as theme park tickets (park admission prices have been given excluding tax in this book). Expect an 11.5 percent tax to be added to bills at Orlando hotels, 13 percent at Kissimmee hotels.

TELEPHONES

Public telephones take coins only. It will cost around 50 cents to make a local call, considerably more for non-local calls (some numbers within the same area code are not considered local; the *White Pages* lists numbers that are local and those that are not) and long-distance calls. Cheaper, off-peak hours are 6–8pm. Some of the budget hotels offer free local calls. The cheapest way to make long-distance and international calls is to buy a phone card, sold in denominations of $5, $10, and $20, at convenience stores; to make a call, you ring an access number and enter the PIN on the back of your card.

TIME

Orlando is on Eastern Standard Time (EST), five hours behind Greenwich Mean Time.

TIPPING

Generally, you should tip 15–20 percent in a restaurant, 15 percent for a taxi, a dollar or two for valet parking and $1 per item carried by a hotel porter. This is not an exhaustive list, however, and tips will be expected in a variety of other situations.

Travel store

Rough Guides travel..

...music & reference

Cuba
Dominican Republic
Dominican Republic
  DIRECTIONS
Ecuador
Guatemala
Jamaica
Mexico
Peru
St Lucia
South America
Trinidad & Tobago
Yúcatan

**AFRICA & MIDDLE
  EAST**

Cape Town & the
  Garden Route
Egypt
The Gambia
Jordan
Kenya
Marrakesh
  DIRECTIONS
Morocco
South Africa,
  Lesotho &
  Swaziland
Syria
Tanzania
Tunisia
West Africa
Zanzibar

**TRAVEL THEME
  GUIDES**

First-Time Around
  the World
First-Time Asia
First-Time Europe
First-Time Latin
  America
Travel Online
Travel Health
Travel Survival
Walks in London &
  SE England
Women Travel

MAPS

Algarve
Amsterdam
Andalucia & Costa
  del Sol

Argentina
Athens
Australia
Baja California
Barcelona
Berlin
Boston
Brittany
Brussels
California
Chicago
Corsica
Costa Rica &
  Panama
Crete
Croatia
Cuba
Cyprus
Czech Republic
Dominican Republic
Dubai & UAE
Dublin
Egypt
Florence & Siena
Florida
France
Frankfurt
Germany
Greece
Guatemala & Belize
Hong Kong
Iceland
Ireland
Kenya
Lisbon
London
Los Angeles
Madrid
Mallorca
Marrakesh
Mexico
Miami & Key West
Morocco
New England
New York City
New Zealand
Northern Spain
Paris
Peru
Portugal

Prague
Rome
San Francisco
Sicily
South Africa
South India
Sri Lanka
Tenerife
Thailand
Toronto
Trinidad & Tobago
Tuscany
Venice
Washington DC
Yucatán Peninsul

**DICTIONARY
  PHRASEBOOKS**

Croatian
Czech
Dutch
Egyptian Arabic
European
  Languages
  (Czech, French,
  German,
  Greek, Italian,
  Portuguese,
  Spanish)
French
German
Greek
Hindi & Urdu
Hungarian
Indonesian
Italian
Japanese
Latin American
  Spanish
Mandarin Chinese
Mexican Spanish
Polish
Portuguese
Russian
Spanish
Swahili
Thai
Turkish
Vietnamese

MUSIC GUIDES

The Beatles
Bob Dylan

Cult Pop
Classical Music
Elvis
Frank Sinatra
Heavy Metal
Hip-Hop
Jazz
Opera
Reggae
Rock
World Music (2 vols)

**REFERENCE
  GUIDES**

Babies
Books for Teenagers
Children's Books,
  0–5
Children's Books,
  5–11
Comedy Movies
Conspiracy Theories
Cult Fiction
Cult Football
Cult Movies
Cult TV
The Da Vinci Code
Ethical Shopping
Gangster Movies
Horror Movies
iPods, iTunes &
  Music Online
The Internet
James Bond
Kids' Movies
Lord of the Rings
Macs & OS X
Muhammad Ali
Music Playlists
PCs and Windows
Poker
Pregnancy & Birth
Sci–Fi Movies
Shakespeare
Superheroes
Unexplained
  Phenomena
The Universe
Weather
Website Directory

Don't bury your head in the sand!

Take cover!

with Rough Guide Travel Insurance

Worldwide cover, for Rough Guide readers worldwide

Check the web at
www.roughguidesinsurance.com

UK: 0800 083 9507
US: 1-800 749-4922
Australia: 1 300 669 999
Worldwide: **(+44) 870 890 2843**

Small print & Index

SMALL PRINT

A Rough Guide to Rough Guides

Orlando DIRECTIONS is published by Rough Guides. The first *Rough Guide to Greece*, published in 1982, was a student scheme that became a publishing phenomenon. The immediate success of the book – with numerous reprints and a Thomas Cook prize short-listing – spawned a series that rapidly covered dozens of destinations. Rough Guides had a ready market among low-budget backpackers, but soon also acquired a much broader and older readership that relished Rough Guides' wit and inquisitiveness as much as their enthusiastic, critical approach. Everyone wants value for money, but not at any price. Rough Guides soon began supplementing the "rougher" information about hostels and low-budget listings with the kind of detail on restaurants and quality hotels that independent-minded visitors on any budget might expect, whether on business in New York or trekking in Thailand. These days the guides offer recommendations from shoestring to luxury and cover a large number of destinations around the globe, including almost every country in the Americas and Europe, more than half of Africa and most of Asia and Australasia. Rough Guides now publish:

- Travel guides to more than 200 worldwide destinations
- Dictionary phrasebooks to 22 major languages
- Maps printed on rip-proof and waterproof Polyart™ paper
- Music guides running the gamut from Opera to Elvis
- Reference books on topics as diverse as the Weather and Shakespeare
- World Music CDs in association with World Music Network

Visit **www.roughguides.com** to see our latest publications.

Publishing information

This first edition published February 2006 by
Rough Guides Ltd, 80 Strand, London WC2R 0RL.
345 Hudson St, 4th Floor, New York, NY 10014, USA.
14 Local Shopping Centre, Panchsheel Park, New Delhi 110017, India.
Distributed by the Penguin Group
Penguin Books Ltd, 80 Strand, London WC2R 0RL
Penguin Group (USA), 375 Hudson Street, New York, NY 10014, USA
Penguin Group (Australia), 250 Camberwell Road, Camberwell, Victoria 3124, Australia
Penguin Group (Canada), 10 Alcorn Avenue, Toronto, ON M4V 1E4, Canada
Penguin Group (New Zealand), Cnr Rosedale and Airborne Roads, Albany, Auckland, New Zealand
Typeset in Bembo and Helvetica to an original design by Henry Iles.
Printed and bound in China

192pp includes index

A catalogue record for this book is available from the British Library

ISBN-13: 978-1-84353-532-4

ISBN-10: 1-84353-532-7

The publishers and authors have done their best to ensure the accuracy and currency of all the information in **Orlando DIRECTIONS**, however, they can accept no responsibility for any loss, injury, or inconvenience sustained by any traveler as a result of information or advice contained in the guide.

1   3   5   7   9   8   6   4   2

Help us update

We've gone to a lot of effort to ensure that the first edition of **Orlando DIRECTIONS** is accurate and up-to-date. However, things change – places get "discovered", opening hours are notoriously fickle, restaurants and rooms raise prices or lower standards. If you feel we've got it wrong or left something out, we'd like to know, and if you can remember the address, the price, the phone number, so much the better.

We'll credit all contributions, and send a copy of the next edition (or any other DIRECTIONS guide or Rough Guide if you prefer) for the best letters. Everyone who writes to us and isn't already a subscriber will receive a copy of our full-color thrice-yearly newsletter. Please mark letters: **"Orlando DIRECTIONS Update"** and send to: Rough Guides, 80 Strand, London WC2R 0RL, or Rough Guides, 4th Floor, 345 Hudson St, New York, NY 10014. Or send an email to **mail@roughguides.com**

Have your questions answered and tell others about your trip at **www.roughguides.atinfopop.com**

Rough Guide credits

Text editor: AnneLise Sorensen
Layout: Umesh Aggarwal, Daniel May
Photography: Demetrio Carrasco
Cartography: Karobi Gogoi, Katie Lloyd-Jones, Maxine Repath

Picture editors: Mark Thomas, Simon Bracken
Proofreader: Diane Margolis
Production: Julia Bovis
Design: Henry Iles
Cover design: Chloë Roberts

The author

Ross Velton is a full-time travel writer. He is the co-author of the *Rough Guide to Florida* and the *Rough Guide to South America* and has contributed to the Rough Guides to Trinidad and Tobago, Mexico, New England, and Brittany and Normandy. He has also authored guidebooks to Haiti and the Dominican Republic, Mali, Mozambique, and Cap d'Agde (the world's largest nudist resort) for other publishers.

Acknowledgements

The author would like to give special thanks to AnneLise Sorensen at Rough Guides, Amy Voss at the Orlando Convention and Visitors Bureau, and Abigail Montpelier at the Kissimmee-St Cloud Convention and Visitors Bureau.

Help was also provided by the following people: David Messina, Lori Babb, Dawn Grigsby, Cara Allen, Susan Storey, Kelly Earnest, Judy Lee, Nadine DeGenova, Mary Kenny, Odalys Aponte, Paul Steiner, Lauren Skowyra, Monica Johnson, and Sherry Major.

Photo credits

All images © Rough Guides except the following:

Front cover: EPCOT dome © Alamy
Back cover: Magic Kingdom's Mad Tea Party Ride © Corbis
p.13 Cirque du Soleil © Network Photographers/Alamy
p.13 Orlando Ballet © Michael Cairns
p.13 Bach Festival © courtesy of the Bach Festival
p.21 Daytona 500 © Transtock Inc/Alamy
p.21 Dwight Howard, Orlando Magic © 2005 NBAE/Fernando Medina/Getty Images

p.26 Gay couple at Walt Disney World © Scott Audette/Corbis Sygma
p.35 Newborn baby © Dorling Kindersley
p.44 Daytona Bike Week © Patrick Ward/Corbis
p.45 Tiger Woods in Orlando © Scott A. Miller/ZUMA/Corbis
p.46 Cypress Cove Nudist Resort & Spa © courtesy of Cypress Cove

Index

Maps are marked in **color**

r